Are You Sure You Want to be a Paralegal? Read This First!

CONTENTS

Acknowledgments

Introduction...

1. Why is the Law Firm Such a Toxic Environment?

2. Why is the Field Bad for Women? / Do You Have the Necessary Character Traits to Make it?

3. The Real Deal on Salary

4. What Litigators Think of Paralegals and What Your Life Will Be

Exhibit 1: *Decoding the Job Advertisement...*

Exhibit 2: *Working with Associates (a/k/a What's That Smell?)...*

Exhibit 3: *Sorry Payroll Didn't Go Through. I was skiing the Swiss Alps...*

Exhibit 4: *We Talked About Giving Bonuses. I Assumed They Went Through. Sorry about that...*

Exhibit 5: *The 24 Hour Move...*

Exhibit 6: *Hauling Water...*

Exhibit 7: *A Tale of Monumental Egos...*

Exhibit 8: *Sex, Drugs, Rock 'N Roll aka I'm Just a Dirty Old Man...*

Exhibit 9: *I Know it's the Friday Before Christmas... I Just Need You to...*

Exhibit 10: *While You're on Vacation, Could You...*

Exhibit 11: *You're a Useless Moron Because You Can't Read My Mind...*

Exhibit 12: *An Assortment of RPP...*

Exhibit 13: *I'm Standing at the Ticket Counter at Delta. Can You Call and Reschedule My Flight?...*

Exhibit 14: *You Know that Conference I Didn't Tell You I was Attending? Where am I Staying?...*

Exhibit 15: *It's 11:45 p.m. I Need You to Respond to This Urgent Email...*

Exhibit 16: *Don't F*** it Up...*

Exhibit 17: *Whatever it Takes, Make it Happen...*

Exhibit 18: *Hi. I'm in Bermuda. Our insurance expires today. Make it Magic!...*

Exhibit 19: *It's 4:00 on the Friday before Labor Day. Surprise! You can Leave Early. Oh, and the Office Will be Closed on Monday (a/k/a My Time & Money Are Valuable, But Yours Aren't)...*

Exhibit 20: *Let's Schedule a Call / Meeting on That...*

Exhibit 21: *We Need to... Why Don't We... Let's...*

Exhibit 22: *I Know It's the 4th of July and You're Getting Your Son From College Today But Can You Just?*

Exhibit 23: *But I want it...*

Exhibit 24: *No Money for File Clerks or Bonuses. But Plenty of Money for Clowns...*

Exhibit 25: *You Haven't Sacrificed Enough...*

5. Survival Tips

Closing Remarks

Copyright © 2023
ISBN: 978-1-312-30782-7
All rights reserved. No part of this publication may be reproduced, distributed, or transmitted in any form or by any means, including photocopying, recording, or other electronic or mechanical methods, without the prior written permission of the Author. Printed in the United States of America. For information, address: https://www.recoveringparalegal.com

ACKNOWLEDGMENTS

I must sincerely thank every attorney I have ever worked for. Without you, this book certainly would not exist.

INTRODUCTION

When you get to the marked exhibits, you are going to think I am making this up. I assure you, I am not.

I worked as a litigation paralegal for nearly ten years (for more than one firm) before I finally had enough. Some might read this and think I just had some bad experiences and am now launching a bitter tirade. This is not so. I actually look back and laugh. In fact, I did not even realize the full extent of the insanity and damage that I had done to myself and my relationships until I quit and walked away. It is my opinion that every law firm is a toxic environment and I will tell you why.

If you are thinking about becoming a litigation paralegal, it is my wish that you read my story and consider it carefully before you embark on your own journey. An associate attorney once asked me how I became a paralegal. I cocked my head sideways for a few seconds before I automatically blurted out without a filter: "It is like getting cancer, it just happens to you." Winding up as a paralegal in a law firm is no place to wind up. Do you remember the 1980's anti-drug campaign message about "Nobody ever says I want to be a junkie when I grow up?" If you are too young to remember that, Google it. Well, just like becoming a junkie, nobody ever says they want to be a paralegal when they grow up. If it happens to you because of poor life choices, you most certainly will not state that you wish to remain a paralegal for your entire working life. Simply stated, friends don't let friends become paralegals.

If you are currently working as a litigation paralegal, it is my wish that this book either provides you with some comic relief, or lights a fire under you to make a change.

Maybe you are happy in your job, and will merely be able to relate to me via our shared experiences.

Being a litigation paralegal means you must have a servant's heart. If you are at all ambitious or even have a basic human desire to exercise some control over your own life, choose another field. There are various schools of thought on this piece of advice. Some will tell you that it is an excellent career choice for women, with steady hours and good income. Mostly the schools will tell you this when they are trying to sell you an expensive, useless, program. I will tell you my thoughts on why this is in fact, a terrible field for women, and I will provide some tips on how to most accurately determine what kind of salary you can realistically expect to earn.

The problem with working too long as a paralegal is that it seems to brand your resume and it is very tough to exit the field and move on to something in another field that can actually make you real money if that is your end goal. As a paralegal, your income is eventually going to be capped and you will wake up and realize that you have actually chosen a dead-end job. I wish someone would have told me that ten years ago. The only way to get ahead in this country is to create something and work for yourself or to get into a real business. If you must work for someone, work for someone who is making an actual product that the public wants to buy. You will never get anywhere working sixty-hour weeks in a law firm for someone else. The dream of going to college and graduating with honors and exchanging this useless piece of paper for a job with a good company that pays you a living wage has long been dead. There is no such thing as loyalty. Corporatism is dead. You are not going to be able to hitch your star to a partner and be taken care of as long as you show up and try on a daily basis. Everyone is disposable now (even the lawyers), and this is one of the most cutthroat businesses that you could ever choose.

If you are currently working for a firm as a litigation paralegal, whatever your reasons may be, you may still think that a dead-end job is actually a good fit for you, and that is certainly possible. If it is, then that is great. If you are happy, well, then, congratulations. That is completely the point, anyway, isn't it? However, if you are wondering what comes next after a few years of slaving away as a paralegal in a law firm, the answer is most likely – NOTHING! You are not going to put your years of service in and make lawyer. If you are in a large firm, you could be promoted to a Paralegal Manager position, but that is probably about it. Of course, life and opportunities are what you create for yourself, and there are very few rules written in stone. Maybe you will become a litigation paralegal who makes $175,000+ a year, is respected by your team, and is completely happy and fulfilled in your position. If that is the case, please drop me a line and tell me where you work!

For me, being a litigation paralegal was something that was fun, exciting, and challenging in my twenties. You know, that time in your life when you are fresh out of college and still trying to figure out who you are and where you fit in the world? That time in your life when you really don't know any better? By the time I was thirty, I was starting to get burned out by all the nonsense that came with the job, and wanted more for my life. I sank deeper into my own self-created psychological hell and watched my life, detached from it, as though I was making a clinical observation. How had my young, promise-filled life turned into something I was trying to survive instead of something I was actively participating in and receiving joy from? There must be something else to life. Something more than scheduling depositions, only to cancel them and re-schedule them. Make the travel plans, cancel the travel plans, over and over again. Revise the brief, circulate the brief, finalize the brief, circulate the brief, revise the brief, etc. I think you get the picture. It takes a certain personality to be happy in a dead-end job.

I knew I was reaching the end of my rope when my brand new boss told me how to get around the low base salary was to put in a bunch of overtime hours. He told me: "I want to see how hard you can work." That's the type of thing you do in your early twenties when you are out to prove to yourself and the world who you are and what you are capable of. My first thought when I heard that line was: "Why don't I just try to find a better job?!" I knew immediately that the best thing I could do in the long run was take those 20 hours of available overtime and instead go home and sit in my office and use that time to invest in myself to further my education and pursue another goal so I could escape that hell pit once and for all!

The purpose of this book is to share my experiences with you so you can get a real look at what it means to work with litigators and what litigation is truly like on a daily basis. I want you to understand what these litigators really think of their paralegals, and the hell that they will put you through in exchange for a sometimes actual living wage. Hopefully, it will even get you thinking about what it means to work as an employee. It will at least give you a good idea of what you might be getting into. Some of the things I experienced I am sure were unique to some of the attorneys I worked for (the holiday notices, or lack thereof, for instance). Other things are rife throughout the entire field, especially the tendency towards vampirism and the complete failure to communicate (you'll see).

In any event, I hope you enjoy the crash course. This is a tell all, I am not holding anything back! I have changed names, dates, and places for my own attempt at protection.

When possible, I have tried to include an email string marked as an exhibit as a real life example of the insanity inside a law firm. I believe these are the best way of portraying the reality of law firm life. As they say, let the documents speak for themselves.

Do not forget to pick up one of the standard t-shirts that are issued to all new hires:

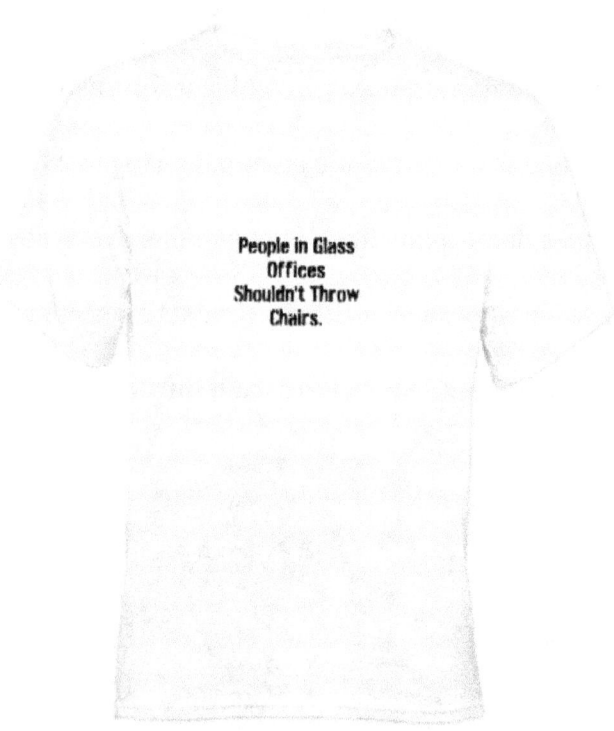

[Note that the uniform apparel became standard issue only after the most recent chair throwing episode by Big Shot New Attorney]

ONE

WHY IS THE LAW FIRM SUCH A TOXIC ENVIRONMENT?

To begin, we should take a good, hard, sobering (ahem) look at the personality characteristics of litigators.

Who Are Your Bosses?

- **Alcoholics**

Psychology Today weighed in on the subject and concluded that: "The ABA estimates that 15-20 percent of all U.S. lawyers suffer from alcoholism or substance abuse." (http://www.psychologytoday.com/blog/therapy-matters/201105/the-depressed-lawyer). To put this number in perspective, consider that The National Institute on Alcohol Abuse and Alcoholism estimates the rate of alcoholism among the general population as 7-10 percent.

The American Bar Association reports that "as many as one in five lawyers is a problem drinker – twice the national rate." (http://www.americanbar.org/groups/lawyer_assistance/resources/alcohol_abuse_dependence.html)

As late as October 29, 2014, The International Journal of Law and Psychiatry study is still being quoted to measure rates of problem drinking as 18 percent for lawyers who have practiced anywhere from 2-20 years, and a whopping 25 percent for lawyers who have been working for 20 or more years. (http://www.chicagolawbulletin.com/Elements/pages/print.aspx?printpath=/Archives/2014/10/29/Alcoholism-Survey-10-29-14&classname=tera.gn3article).

Working for alcoholics can potentially make your work life completely toxic and dysfunctional for obvious reasons, but consider this. What if being in an environment for years on end where the culture encourages and feeds toxicity starts to affect you? What you are exposed to on a daily basis becomes your normal sense of reality. Functioning among bosses who forget everything they ever told you <u>and</u> forget to tell you key pieces of information you need to know to do your job (but then punish you for not knowing what they forgot to tell you), will make you a nervous wreck or an alcoholic yourself. For a few years, I was probably both. I honestly did not realize how toxic my job was until a few months after I quit drinking myself. That subject is probably best reserved for another book entirely.

- **Unhappiest Workers in America**

In that same Psychology Today article that is linked above, it is reported that a Johns Hopkins University Study found that lawyers have the highest rates of depression among more than 100 different occupations. Careerbliss.com routinely puts out a study about the happiest / unhappiest jobs in America and guess what tops the list for unhappiest? Associate Attorney! Also worth mentioning is the fact that Legal Assistant was closely followed as the Number 7 Unhappiest Job in America. In my mind, it should be ranked right behind Associate Attorney. (http://www.careerbliss.com/facts-and-figures/careerbliss-happiest-and-unhappiest-jobs-in-america-2013/). For more commentary on the unhappiest jobs in America please read: http://abovethelaw.com/2013/03/unhappiest-job-in-america-take-a-guess/

http://www.businessinsider.com/unhappiest-jobs-in-america-2013-12

http://www.forbes.com/pictures/efkk45ehffl/no-1-unhappiest-job-associate-attorney/

- **Assholes**

There are plenty of attorney jokes. The hard data to back it up might be found in Bob Sutton's *The No Asshole Rule: Building a Civilized Workplace and Surviving One That Isn't*. It will come as no surprise to anyone in the field that the legal field is an occupation that is rife with overbearing assholes who engage in constant psychological abuse towards their staff members and co-workers. They may do it by assigning demeaning, meaningless "emergency" tasks that chip away at your spirit little by little, or they may do it in obvious ways such as barking at you like a dog in front of their clients for you to fetch things. Jennifer Alvey also explains clearly and concisely just what it is that makes lawyers such assholes. To find her explanation, visit:

http://leavinglaw.wordpress.com/2014/05/16/why-are-there-so-many-asshole-lawyers/.

- **Psychopaths**

Kevin Dutton's *The Wisdom of Psychopaths: What Saints, Spies and Serial Killers can Teach us About Success*, lists lawyers as second on the list of occupations that attract the most psychopaths. This is completely believable and certainly comes as no surprise to me. As an employee, the factors that you should be the most concerned about are detachment and lack of empathy. What do you think it will do to you on a daily basis to interact with someone who fails to exhibit human emotions and normal characteristics? I promise you the result is not going to make your life better.

(http://www.abajournal.com/news/article/the_legal_field_attracts_psychopaths_author_says_not_that_there_is_anything/)

(http://www.businessinsider.com/most-psychopathic-professions-2012-11)

Now you at least know who you will be working for. But what does it really mean? Name calling is great, but what exactly are all these alcoholic, depressed and unhappy, asshole psychopaths going to do to you to make your sheer existence a living nightmare? Let me count the ways.

Why/How the Work Itself is Toxic

Here are my best explanations for how the law firm turns into a practical nightmare for the paralegal.

- **Your Work Isn't Meaningful**

There are so many studies that support the idea that most workers just want the chance to be engaged in something that matters. (http://www.washingtonpost.com/national/on-leadership/how-to-completely-utterly-destroy-an-employees-work-life/2012/03/05/gIQAxU3iuR_story.html). Paralegals certainly fit this characteristic. You start out bright-eyed and optimistic at the law firm, thinking that you are going to do good work and make a valuable contribution. You might work like a dog to get a case shaped up and actually achieve that goal of making a valuable contribution. Then, the partners will do one of the most demoralizing things that they can do to a paralegal, which is arbitrarily reassign teams and you will watch as your work disappears to another team, and the lazy paralegal who inherits all the work and research you did will get the credit for your hard work and contribution. Your reward is that you get to keep your job and do it all over again from scratch. Congratulations on your hard work and effort. No one cares what you did, what you are doing, and what you are going to do. Just shut up and keep the seat warm.

- **When Everything is an Emergency**

Paralegals have natural tendencies to be helpful and they want nothing more than to make themselves part of a dynamic team. Does the paralegal need to find last minute evidence to support an issue? That paralegal will turn the world upside down to find an article from an expert that is out of print, locate a missing witness, or manufacture a last minute demonstrative exhibit. One of the things I always used to hear from litigators is that they have no control over last minute and emergency tasks. I do not know who they think they are talking to because I have worked alongside them, and my observation is that emergency tasks are usually due to the person in charge failing to plan. I get it if the opposing side springs an emergency motion on us, but otherwise it should not come as a surprise to anyone that in twenty or thirty days we are going to have to respond to discovery requests or file a response to a motion. When your boss refuses to sit back and count backwards from the deadline and get the employees mobilized so they can have the time and tools they need to help the best they can, you are looking at living in a pressure cooker reality where every single work day is on a deadline. This is an awful, unproductive way to live and is actually a complete disservice to the clients you are supposed to be working for in the first place. If you find yourself in a situation where you are constantly being made to work overtime and stay late because of a failure to plan by your superiors, you are in a toxic law firm. If you are in a firm where you arrive at work at 8:00 a.m. every morning, but your boss does not assign you work for the day until 4:00 or 4:30, you need to find another job before this completely kills your spirit and motivation.

Being asked to deal with non-emergencies when you are supposed to be on vacation is completely demoralizing as well. These assignments will usually begin with "While you are on vacation, can you just…" The best way to respond to this is: "Um, are you serious right now (coupled with an eyebrow raise)?" Employers need to realize that employees need vacations to recharge and nurture relationships. Having some time away from the daily stresses of litigation will allow workers time to actually be creative and come up with innovations on how to do their jobs better! Time off makes people happier. Happier people come back to work fired up and motivated and are able to be better workers who produce better work product. The good employers (and real businesses) do realize this as truth.

When last minute real emergencies occur, employees on a healthy team will voluntarily stay with bosses as long as they need to, and willingly pitch in. However, when employees start to feel that they are being taken advantage of and that their time is being disrespected, this will start chipping away at morale and contribute to the toxicity level. Unfortunately, though, litigator psychopath bosses just do not care about making the environment better for their clients and members of their own staff.

- **Unrealistic Expectations**

This is where the lawyer gives the paralegal responsibilities beyond the average five-year associate at a big firm and basically says "Good luck. Don't f*** it up." Sometimes it is funny, and you can think of it as a sort of hazing exercise to separate the men from the boys. Other times it is sheer insanity, and it really is not acceptable to put non-lawyers under that kind of pressure. I know a lawyer who sent his paralegal to the hospital before trial because of heart palpitations. She was in her late twenties and demonstrating symptoms of a heart attack. Remember – telling a paralegal "Don't f*** it up" is not a reasonable job expectation.

- **No Communication or Poor Communication**

ESP CANNOT BE A REAL JOB REQUIREMENT

It should not be a job requirement that your employees must read minds. I am serious, I have actually overheard more than one partner tell an associate that he was useless because he could not read his mind. This is the type of psychological torture and abuse that runs rampant in law firms, and it is absolute bullshit to me and should be to you too. The bosses are either too lazy, just don't care, or actually want to emotionally abuse you because they get off on it. I don't care what the reasoning is for this completely unacceptable type of behavior. As a caveat, after being in the real business world, I can tell you that real CEO's do not operate this way. High caliber business teams do not operate this way. People working in real businesses, doing real work, do not have time to bullshit around. This is a lawyer "thing." I define a "real" business as working in an industry that has a main goal of creating a product or service that people want to buy as opposed to working in an industry that seems to have as its main goal the sole end game of billing someone for some bullshit you made up to do for the sake of creating a bill to send to someone so they would pay you for your so-called services.

LAWYERS HATE TO BE SPECIFIC AND THEY REALLY HATE BEING CLEAR AND CONCISE

Everything is as difficult and complicated as you let them make it. What would make the most sense for everyone involved with the work, would be if the boss would sit back and think about what it is that he actually wants to accomplish, and then communicate that in a clear and concise manner to the employees. But that is almost NEVER what happens. Lawyers hate giving specific, clear instructions. For instance, lawyers like to make lazy edicts to notice the depositions of "all fact witnesses," without sitting back and thinking about the people he really wants to depose. When the associate and paralegal get together and send out twenty deposition notices to all the fact witnesses, the boss lawyer will have a tantrum because of the volume and cost. Why? Because what he really meant to do was, of course, *only depose all fact witnesses who are likely to have the most relevant information pertaining to the important details of the case.* The seasoned paralegal knows this, but the sniveling baby associate lawyer is terrified of leaving a witness out. So we start spinning our wheels, our money, our very souls, and work until the point of exhaustion on useless, meaningless tasks, sending deposition notices out to "witnesses" who know nothing: the police officer who signed off on the investigating officer's report; the co-pilot of the EMS flight; and on and on.

Why not spend a few minutes brainstorming the witness list and then just let the paralegal prepare the deposition notices one time? Why do they make things so hard?! It seems so simple and effective. Reflect, and then decide. The lawyers will not do it. They like to bill for useless crap projects and run for the sake of running without accomplishing anything real. They make their money on perpetuating bullshit and making things harder than they have to be. That's their trade. You can't show up and start trying to be efficient, silly paralegal! You are messing with their profit margin!

CONSTANT INTERRUPTIONS

Some bosses like to run in to their employee's office and tell them about all the different ways of accomplishing a task. For efficiency, the process that would make the most sense would be for the boss to think about it on their own and then reserve a time during the day for staff to meet about priorities and give final assignments, not a list of four different ways we could do something. Great employees just want to do something one way, one time and get it right. Great people do not want to spend their morning digging a ditch and then filling it back up in the afternoon. Remember, every time a worker is interrupted, precious productive time is lost working on other ASAP tasks that you assigned earlier, and ultimately helping the lawyer's clients.

ON REMEMBERING:

Bad bosses in toxic law firms irritate, alienate, and completely frustrate their employees because they fail to pay attention to what is going on. Good bosses listen to employees when they are talking to them.

A Public Service Plea to Asshole bad bosses: Pay attention! We are paying attention to you. And another thing. As a rule, assume that if you did not directly tell someone something then they do not have the information. Some attorneys are in the habit of pretending they told their paralegal to do something, and then they like to get mad when the mysterious something never gets done. Paralegals try their hardest to guard against this phenomenon by looking at the calendar and planning ahead, but from time to time you will have something going on that you failed to tell us about. YOU HAVE TO TELL US THE INFORMATION IF YOU WANT US TO KNOW THE INFORMATION. No more excuses.

GIVING "WE NEED TO DO" ASSIGNMENTS

In a toxic law firm, no one knows what they are supposed to be doing, there is no accountability, and nothing ever really gets done. Lawyers may think that by speaking this way, they are invoking a team atmosphere. All that they are really doing is creating confusion. Assign tasks to specific people! Avoid giving three different people the same assignment or your staff will think you are a moron and start hating you. You are killing your employees when you do this type of stuff.

REFUSING TO LOOK AT EXHIBITS

When the team is preparing a motion, a bad boss comments to the paralegal as he is passing by her desk that she needs to find "that email, you know, the one that is good for us," the attorney is going to need to review what has been pulled before it is filed with the court. The attorney needs to show up and care about the evidence.

YOU CAN IGNORE EVERYONE IN THE WORLD IF YOU WANT TO, BUT NOT YOUR OWN PEOPLE

Toxic bosses refuse to answer emails or questions from their subordinates. Every now and then, paralegals and associates will need clarification on the given assignment. If your boss blatantly ignores you, you are in trouble. The employee is only asking because they are working on helping their law firm's clients and helping them make money. They are not asking questions because they think it is a fun thing to do.

- **Wasting Time and Resources**

This really ties back to the emergency task and meaningful work sections. Again, it is very hard to have a result other than a toxic environment when employees feel that you do not respect their time. One of the biggest time wasters I have seen inside a law office is to have a paralegal draft a memo (and bill for it, mind you) about some simplistic task that needs to be done later that afternoon. WHY? Why are you making me waste time drafting a memo about records that need to be requested this afternoon? Why am I not just going to my office and actually requesting the records that you need? I will tell you why. Because if I did the task without generating the nonsense memo I would be missing out on billing the client 0.20 – 0.40. This adds up to a lot of money throughout the year. Paralegal and Associate 101 - ABB, baby! Always Be Billing. If you are the type of person who just wants to be measured in actual results and productivity, the law firm is not the place for you. The law firm needs good soldiers who will dedicate their lives to creating and billing for work product, not trying to efficiently produce resolutions.

- **Bleeding Your Employees Dry and Refusing to Deal with Things**

Bad bosses like to act like assholes and not show up for appointments and miss phone calls. Then, they make their subordinates deal with the fall out. Another thing that bad bosses will do is ignore a case and hope it goes away. In fact, this is a big strategy for anything they don't feel like dealing with, actually. When it blows up, they will just pawn it off and blame an associate and then have a paralegal clean it up.

- **Not Being Treated as a Professional**

A good boss will recognize that you are an educated professional who has valuable skills to add to the team. A toxic asshole boss will think that you are there only to fetch papers off the printer, bring him coffee, and order his lunch. When you are not doing that, maybe you can make some stickers to affix on folders, and engage in stupid conversations with public workers about why they refuse to produce fact records. If the jerk really starts to trust you, he will start to let you fetch papers off the printer and tab them out into notebooks for him. Then the fun can really begin.

- **When Partners Run Wild**

Every law firm has one. This could be the guy who has graduated from high-functioning alcoholic to sad alcoholic, and is currently on the fast track to disbarment. Or, it could just be the incompetent person who everyone can't believe actually made partner. Perhaps it is the classic mid-life crisis partner who is sleeping with a staff member to feel better about his life. Whatever the story is, the ending is the same. The staff is watching. Any craziness up the chain contributes to bad morale and toxicity levels.

- **What Happens When Employees Don't Have a System to Measure and Reward Their Excellence**

A WORD ON MOTIVATION

The more involved and motivated employees are, the better they are able to intuitively know how to do their jobs and help move the case along without a whole bunch of hand holding from the lawyers. They will also be the type of self-starters who will volunteer for tasks and take on new cases. They will become highly skilled at seizing opportunities to be of service to the firm and the clients in a million little ways that their supervising lawyers will probably never even know about. One of the best ways to keep a paralegal engaged in the case is to let them attend key depositions and hearings. This will save the attorney time as well, but few lawyers actually do this. They could avoid coming back to the office and having to conduct a meeting. The paralegal could be right there when the witness says "We'll look for that and get you a copy," or when the judge tells someone to produce something. Paralegals live for this type of stuff! You need a document? We are all over that! Providing opportunities for the employee to be engaged in the work is the most motivating thing a boss can do to build loyalty and ensure excellent performance.

A paralegal can really be the backbone of the law practice, so if one of them calls something to their lawyer's attention that needs handling, it needs to be handled. Good paralegals try to limit asking questions or bothering the lawyer unless it is absolutely necessary. So if one of them says that they need something (you know, that handful of times every year), the boss needs to make it happen if at all possible. Otherwise, they are just going to zap the motivation right out of the paralegal.

Praise is great, and is appreciated. But nothing shows that you value your employees like the way you pay them. Good firms do not mess this one up. If an extra $5,000 - $10,000 here and there is the difference between keeping your best team intact, and operating at full capacity like the well-oiled machine it is, then managing partners had better ask themselves if they would rather live with or without their current team intact. Remember, it is cheaper to keep good people than incur the replacement costs. Paralegals are not greedy, unreasonable people. But it needs to be understood that they are not at the law firm for the purposes of doing charity work. Great employees want to contribute and help their lawyers become wildly successful and impressed with the contributions that are made to the firm. Paralegals want to be wildly successful too. You know, but for a paralegal.

A WORD ON RULES

Decide on what type of culture you want your firm to have and if you have an Administrator, let that person be responsible for communicating and enforcing that culture. But be careful with the rules you create. Rules are for people who do not know how to act appropriately, so it begs the question of why you are hiring them in the first place. Why not just hire good, responsible, professional people and let them do their jobs? The moment performance becomes a problem, start hammering down, but until then, why not let adults police themselves? Paralegals in general do not make it a habit of engaging in activities that do not make sense to them. So make all the rules you want, but I am telling you that you are going to have a compliance and morale problem if you are making them for the sake of making them. And especially, if millennial paralegals (workers born between 1980 and 2000) are taking over your office. Good luck with that.

I understand that in a bigger organization there is an increased need to manage people. But your Administrator needs to understand that when one of the firm's most profitable paralegals, who just billed as much as one of the top partners did last month when they were on trial, is not going to answer her when she calls (interrupting billable work, I might add) to ask why the paralegal took an hour and 15-minute lunch one time this month. The Administrator can go pound sand. Actually, probably the best thing the Administrator can do when it comes to a reliable and profitable employee, is change her mind about her perceived need to discuss any matter with the employee. From the paralegal's perspective, they are worried about their team. If the paralegal is taking care of their team, they are fulfilling their role within the firm. There is really nothing that the Administrator and the excellent employee need to discuss, and it is appreciated if the supervising attorney has the employee's back and makes that known once they have proven themselves to be worthy of that trust.

A WORD ON BONUSES

Let me paint this picture for you. Take Paralegal "A." This Paralegal always has some type of crazy drama going in her life that prevents her from working a full week. EVER. This girl has no idea what a forty-hour workweek looks like. There is one in every firm, it seems. Now, compare her with Paralegal "B." Paralegal "B" never pawns her work off on her co-workers, and consistently volunteers to take on more cases and help prepare for more depositions, hearings, and trials. She has a good attitude, is smart and ambitious, you know she cares about the clients, and other people in the office have fun working with her. You count on her as sure as the sun rises in the morning. Who do you think should get a bonus? If you think that both of them should get the same bonus, you are dead wrong.

When you get an employee who goes above and beyond, consistently volunteering to take on more responsibilities and shoulder the burden for another co-worker, you need to reward that type of behavior with a bonus that is enough to motivate them to keep doing what they do. To do otherwise completely kills Paralegal "B's" spirit. Why keep killing yourself going above and beyond when no one seems to notice? The cold hard truth about bonuses is that if the firm is toxic it really won't matter too much how much you pay your employees, because it will never be enough. Employees are wising up, and the American culture is finally moving towards realizing that money will never equal happiness. More and more employees are reaching the conclusion that they are unable to sell their health, happiness, emotional well-being, quality of life, and sacrificed relationships for a high enough price. This is becoming increasingly clear at the paralegal price point! Associates may be fooled a little bit longer because they may stay to keep chasing the elusive partner track carrot. A paralegal is the only job I know where a person can sacrifice everything that matters in their personal life to advance a trial team's goal of winning millions and be the only person in the room who drives off in a Chevy Cobalt to eat a peanut butter sandwich at home because pay day is still two days off. Don't be a chump in exchange for a paycheck!

I used to see it all around me in the law firm. A toxic law firm creates a system where co-workers will act busier than they are in order to avoid incurring additional responsibility "dumps." The firm actively kills ambition and motivation because there is no system in place to reward high achievers. After you have been at a firm for awhile you will start to notice how the lifers do not volunteer for new projects anymore. They pawn off cases to new employees. These people are hell to work with now, but in the beginning they were bright-eyed and optimistic just like the newbie coming in who raises her hand and volunteers, under the mistaken belief that they are building a name and reputation that will lead to good things down the line. Unfortunately, after a year or two, the honeymoon wears off and the employee is beaten down from being rewarded with more work. Their excellent work ethic that they came into the firm with takes a hit because they are tired of their co-workers dumping work on them. The once excellent employee starts to resent the toxic system and this person turns into someone who is just trying to survive the day. Firms could avoid all of this toxicity if they just cared enough to have someone monitor the work loads and establish a performance program. But they don't, because they don't care how hard they make your life everyday. If you don't like it, you can quit. There will always be someone else to come along and do your job. In fact, I am convinced that is the intent of their business model. They do it with associates fresh out of law school. They work them like slave labor and suck everything that is good out of them until they quit. Then, they just start over with fresh meat.

A job at a toxic law firm will most likely ultimately result in you being turned into an alcoholic (or medicated zombie); a depressed person; a nervous wreck; or an asshole bully who interrogates the people in your life. I have known hundreds of paralegals over the years in all types of different firms, and the result is always the same. The people who profess to be happy are the same people who take antidepressants or anxiety medication just to function in their daily lives. They are not living life, they are numb to life so they can survive and keep getting a paycheck. They are stuck in a dead-end job and have self-medicated to the point where they gave up the fight long ago. It is a sad, sad result. These people are blind to reality. To read more about toxic companies visit:

http://www.fastcompany.com/35667/dangertoxic-company.

TWO

WHY IS THE FIELD BAD FOR WOMEN? / DO YOU HAVE THE NECESSARY CHARACTER TRAITS TO MAKE IT?

Not to deter male paralegals from purchasing my book, but the vast majority of paralegals are women. I have seen a mix of paralegals in my experience and what I have noticed is that the two biggest groups of women paralegals are comprised of what I will call for simplicity purposes Type "A" and Type "B" people.

The classic Type "A's" are the super ambitious people who make their career goals more important than their personal lives. Their work ethics mirror their boss. They generally have great analytical and critical thinking skills. They are (as lawyers like to say, "smart enough to go to law school"). I myself was defined as this type, but believe me this is no badge of honor. These people have graduated with honors from a four-year university and usually have some sort of extended continuing legal education. Inevitably, these workers will find that they cannot be happy with their dead-end jobs (Cambridge Dictionaries Online defines a dead-end job as: "a job in which there is no chance of progressing to a better, more important job" – so you tell me if that doesn't just nail what a paralegal is) and will ultimately fight to pursue another career path or they will resign themselves to becoming one of those high-functioning alcoholics or self-medicated people because they cannot break out of the trap. The drudgery, coupled with the humble servant's attitude you are forced to take on to keep your job, combined with the repetitive and mind-numbing tasks will drive the Type "A" person insane.

The Type "B" paralegal is the person who really just wants to find a steady good-paying job so they can contribute to their household. This very well could be a single mother or a wife. This classification of worker may be ambitious enough and smart enough to desire more than a dead-end paralegal job, but because this person places more value on family, personal relationships, and probably their own health, they do not want to pursue law school. Sooner or later, they realize that they are in hell but they just resign themselves to the mantra of "I am doing what I have to do to take care of my family. After all, everyone has to work, right?"

Ultimately, my argument that the field is bad for women is based on the observation that it can kill the work ethic of the Type "A" paralegal and will inevitably beat down the Type "B." When the two meet as co-workers, much conflict ensues.

If you are the type of person who takes pride and ownership in your job it can be difficult, frustrating, and demoralizing to be a passive participant in someone else's business. You may have great ideas and input to offer, but your boss will not care because you are just staff. If this bothers you, do not become a paralegal. You have to realize that you are not going to work hard and get stock options or climb to partner level. You are staff – that is all you are ever going to be in a law firm. If this bothers you, you need to become your own boss or at least pick a business that has real growth potential where your talents will be rewarded in accordance with your performance.

If you are okay with just being a replaceable cog in the wheel (just another butt in a seat, quite frankly) who will have to jump on command to squelch so-called emergency fires, then sign right up. But do not go into it blindly. Know that this type of job is how you become a slave and your life feels like a prison. Please know this. No one told me this, and I wish that someone would have told me all those years ago!

Perhaps the best way to find out if your personality is a fit for law firm life is to take my short test. Notice how the language in some of the questions helps demonstrate how the very nature of working in the legal field will hurt relationships between women.

1. You are assigned to a team where one of the single mother paralegals either has to come in late or leave early every week in order to deal with a childcare issue, which means that she is constantly passing her last-minute deadline tasks onto you for you to take care of. This has been going on consistently for the past four months. How does this make you feel?

    a. I'm happy to help out. No drama, complaints, or conflicts from me. I'm practically Mother Theresa. Some people say I get taken advantage of and never stand up for myself. I just have the cat at home, so I like to feel needed by other humans.

    b. What you think in your head: "This bitch needs to get her act together! Why is she creating more stress in my life?! I didn't have kids, yet I am being punished for her decision to have kids?! In what world is this happening?! Why is she making this crap my problem now?! UGH!"

    c. What you tell your best friend downstairs in the bar after you finally left work at 8:00 p.m. after working twelve hours with asshole lawyers: "I'm fixing to kill this bitch. I don't get overtime pay when she dumps stuff on me at the last second to handle. I would go to A. Big Shot Attorney if I thought he gave a rat's ass for two seconds. But I know better than to complain because all they really care about is that someone does the work. They don't care who does it or at what price."

2. Today your job is to print a bunch of unorganized pleadings off the server and create notebooks of filings by chronological order. You will spend the first half of the day doing this project and think you have successfully finished just before lunch. You walk the notebooks back to drop off with the lawyer, and he looks up and says "Oh. I found two more motions a couple of hours ago. Can you just go back and work these in?" This little memory lapse will mean you have to spend another worthless hour or two re-organizing what you thought you were already finished doing. What are you thinking?

    a. Whatever. I'm getting paid right now. If they want me to sit here all day and move papers around in a notebook, that's great. I'm inside. The air-conditioning is working today and I can put my headphones on. I also have health insurance. Aces up! WHATEVER! I'm here until 5:00 p.m. and then I am FREE, FREE, FREE!

   b. I seriously hate this jackass. I'm about to dump this on the new girl or our intern because I don't have time for this crap!

   c. Why do they waste so much time and so many resources?! This job makes me sick! I just want to do a good job where I can actually use my brain and be productive! The fact that he is constantly doing this to me proves that he does not value my time! I HATE THIS PLACE!

3. You overheard your boss on the phone today telling someone "I'll have my paralegal jump and get that for you." Assess your ability to jump.

   a. Good jobs are hard to find. I make $25.00 per hour and that's good enough for me. As long as they aren't asking me to do anything illegal, and I don't have to take my top off for tips, I'm game for whatever I need to do to keep my job. It's just part of life.

   b. That guy is so condescending. I am so sick of hearing him call me "staff," and telling people that I jump to bring him and his associates whatever they command me to bring. I'm just going to get the new girl to do it. She doesn't know any better yet. She'll run in there with a smile and do jumping jacks if I tell her to.

   c. I hate how this guy talks down to me and refuses to use my actual name. I've been working for him for five years! I seriously constantly daydream about the 1980 movie Nine to Five when I am in the office.

4. Your Firm Administrator just sent out a five-page memo detailing her changes to the way your activity will be monitored while you are at work. There is also a new vacation policy that declares that seniority does not mean you are automatically approved to redeem your vacation days to coincide with Christmas Day and Thanksgiving. What's running through your mind when you see this memo?

   a. So, if I'm reading this correctly, we now have to make sure we are signed in five minutes prior to the time we are actually scheduled to start and have our computers running and ready to answer the phone at 8:30, not walking in the door at 8:30. She also wants to make sure we are signing out with her if we leave the office for lunch, if we take a bathroom break, and signing out with her when we go home for the day. I can do that. No problem.

   b. This is how they reward five solid years of reliable hard work?! By treating me as though I am in grade school?! Are you kidding me?! This place is a joke. I better go talk to the Administrator and work a deal. I've got some dirt and it may be time to trade it to make sure this policy doesn't apply to people like me.

    c. The last time I checked I was a free American citizen. I'm working on doing some great things in my life. These great things do not involve spending twenty minutes of my day engaging in some more unnecessary bureaucratic red tape just so that the Administrator can feel that she is doing something to justify her exorbitant salary. Until they convict me and incarcerate me into our prison system, I will not be asking another fellow human being if I am allowed to go visit my family at Christmas. I QUIT! This place is BULLSHIT! I'm not doing it one more second!

5. Your boss just called you into his office and really gave you the old what for about how you screwed something up. The something was basically that he needed some records from a certain facility and you never got them. The problem is that you never knew you were supposed to get these records. The lawyer never told you to, and the client never mentioned their existence. Can you live your life this way?

    a. It doesn't bother me to get berated, belittled, and demeaned for something I never knew I was supposed to be working on. Like I said before, I'm getting paid. I don't care about this guy or this job or even the clients, so long as that check cashes every two weeks. I'm just here to make some money and this guy isn't going to make me feel some type of way.

    b. Typical. I smoothed it over just fine when I expertly lied like a psychopath and told him I was so busy answering discovery that I had to delegate that one little small thing to new girl. I can't believe she didn't take care of it! It just makes me absolutely sick how I can't trust any of my co-workers to do their jobs!

    c. NO. I. REALLY. JUST. CAN'T.

In case it isn't completely obvious to you, only the people who can honestly answer all "a's" belong in the law firm.

THREE

THE REAL DEAL ON SALARY

Without knowing exactly what city your market is located in, it is impossible for me to offer specific salary information for paralegal jobs. However, I urge you to run the numbers from the following websites:

- www.salarysurvey.com
- www.payscale.com
- www.indeed.com
- www.monster.com
- www.ziprecruiter.com

Now, also run the numbers on the other jobs you are considering, or that you even think you might be qualified to do. Watch the job boards and pay attention to what is being offered for what experience level. Are you going to be happier as a restaurant manager making a living wage or as a paralegal scraping by at $50k? I would take the restaurant every single time. No kidding. Most customers are not going to engage you in a fifteen minute interrogation about why it took eight minutes instead of five to get their meal to the table.

You may even get someone in a paralegal association in your city or a few firm administrators who will give you some honest answers if you tell them you are looking at going into the field as an entry-level person. I would not rely on the schools to have the most relevant salary information that is true for your market.

The truth is that the salary starting out for most paralegal jobs is extremely poor, and especially if you are not in a major city. I moved from a major market to a little bit of a smaller market (not so long ago) and the best thing I could find paid about $30k less than I had been used to making. The real problem is that the cost of living was estimated to be exactly the same for both cities, so the change was definitely felt. It just did not make any sense to me in the world to remain in the awful law firm prison when I could make much more money waiting tables for cash tips until I could sort something else out. Yes, I am dead serious right now. In some markets, your four-year degree and almost ten years of heavy responsibility, substantive legal work will net you a whopping $17.00 per hour folks! That is of course, before you pay taxes on it. There are so many other things that you can do with your life besides get paid for wasting time all day. It just seems sad and pointless to get the crap kicked out of you on a daily basis and engage in nonsense just so you can pay <u>almost</u> all of your bills every month. And the real kick in the teeth is that you are not going to be doing anything as a paralegal that really has any real value. You would think at such a low price point that the job might at least have some kind of satisfaction where you would at least get to feel happy about contributing something to the world or an individual client.

Forget it.

At least if you choose to be a worker in a real business you are actually getting paid to build something. As a paralegal, you are getting paid to engage in bullshit for the longest amount of time so the firm can get paid. Keep that in mind. The objective is not to help people. Go be a social worker or a counselor if you think you are going to help people. Paralegals do not help. Some of the lawyers might, but honestly even that is debatable. Your job is to request papers, assemble the papers, and then re-assemble the papers. Nobody is going to care what you think the papers mean. You just make spreadsheets and papers about what information is on what bates-labeled page. I take that back. Maybe, just maybe, around year five, you might be trusted to gather exhibits in support of an issue.

Good for you. You sure are setting the world on fire now!

FOUR

WHAT LITIGATORS THINK OF PARALEGALS AND WHAT YOUR LIFE WILL BE

I would like to open with a few quotes, because they really speak for themselves:

- "Paralegals are an important part of running an effective law practice, but dishwashers are an important part of running a restaurant. It's different, but not so different. It's important to know who you are in the world, but it's rare." - http://www.abajournal.com/mobile/comments/paralegal_peeks_at_part-time_lawyers_check_takes_pay_peeve_to_advice_column

- "The paralegal students I taught, at an ABA-accredited paralegal program, found it hard to understand basic legal concepts, wrote like middle school kids, lacked motivation, and were doing this because they had nothing else to do with their lives. A couple were highly-motivated and smart, but most weren't. Most were rather stupid to be honest. Most just didn't care. The work I graded was embarrassingly bad." http://outsidethelawschoolscam.blogspot.com/2013/04/the-jd-as-sub-paralegal-qualification.html

To lawyers, paralegals are a subservient class of people. They refer to non-lawyers amongst themselves as "regular people." We serve, and we serve quietly with no push back. To do otherwise is to endanger your job. They know it and many employers exploit this position. A sampling of real emails. Remember, I have the original receipts. None of this is manufactured!

> **From: A. Big Shot Attorney**
> **To: Paralegal**
> **Subject: Computer**
>
> Why the fuck is my computer not been fixed. I was gone for a whole week.

From: A. Big Shot Attorney
To: Paralegal
Subject: Filing

I have asked you to get my filing straight. The Tobacco case may be the biggest case in this office and it looks like trash. I have asked multiple times that this file be set up, the documents organized properly etc. I just spent thirty minutes literally looking for the file and it was under a stack of other crap by your desk. Please do not do anything else for anyone until all of my filing is straight.

From: A. Big Shot Attorney
To: Paralegal
Subject: Website and Task

Why is there no case results and stuff on the website still? I have asked you to do this four or five times. It should take five minutes. Do it tomorrow without fail. Also, I still do not have a list of dictation. I don't know what has been sent, typed and now don't even remember what has been dictated. I want all of this done tomorrow.

Please listen to these instructions. If Doug or anyone else asks you to do something, you do not do it until you get my work done. MY WORK comes before anything else you do in this office. Anything. You tell Doug to see me. I do not understand why I do not have the list of the dictation I asked about 10 days ago. I planned to finish all of that up today and now I cannot.

Until I say otherwise, you need a list of tasks that you are to complete. You need to email it to me a couple of days each week. There is too much stuff that is not getting done or that I am having to ask you multiple times about. I understand you are working hard. I have no doubt about that. But, your organization is terrible right now. It may be that you have too much work. Doug can do his own stuff. I am going to talk to him about it tomorrow. At his age, he should not be using assistants and paralegals nearly as much as he is. It is unprofitable and not smart.

From here out, you do my work and my work only unless you have my permission to do something else. Sorry for the terse email but I do not know how to communicate otherwise.

From: A. Big Shot Attorney
To: Paralegal and Legal Assistant
Subject: Smith v. Gulfstream

I don't know or care what the problem is about these scheduling issues and getting stuff on my calendar. You all have to work together. Michelle controls my calendar. She is to put stuff on the paper and e-calendar. This includes dates people tell her to hold. This should really be very simple. I should not have to mess with or even think about this stuff. It may be surprising, but most of the stuff I do is very high stress and complicated. I do not want to hear about this again. There may be other lawyers that do things differently and I do not care. I have more travel and stuff going than anyone else and I want my calendar managed the way I want it managed.

From: A. Big Shot Attorney
To: Paralegal
Sent: Sunday, October 6, 20__ 9:45 a.m.
Subject: Can u come in at 11?

From: A. Big Shot Attorney
To: Paralegal
Subject: My box

Please put everything in my box or in my chair like you have been doing. Someone came in and put a bunch of crap on my desk and it was a complete mess. If someone comes by to drop something for me, take it from them. Thanks.

From: A. Big Shot Attorney
To: Paralegal
Subject: ASAP and Rush Work

In the future, if The Conquistador has something that is pressing and it interferes with something that I need you to do ASAP, then you need to make both of us aware of the conflict. It is not appropriate for you to choose one attorney's work over another attorney's work and/or to refrain from telling the attorney whose work you cannot do, that you are unable to do so. If The Conquistador and I both need something done asap, then we should be asked to decide how to handle it, or you may ask someone else for assistance (to do the tape, for example). But, you cannot simply refrain from telling me that something I thought was being done cannot be done by you. I am busy and cannot remember everything I give to you, and I rely upon you to bring any conflicts in work to my attention or to find someone to assist you so that both attorneys' work can be timely accomplished. **Moreover, you indicated that you would do the tapes asap, but you left for lunch and it was not done.** Please ask me if you need help. If you have any questions, let me know.

From: A. Big Shot Attorney
To: Minion Paralegals
Subject: Thank You

The firm is appreciative of the great brunch prepared by the staff yesterday. The food was delicious and we always enjoy a brief time of relaxation with our staff.
[Note - he can only stand to be around you peons for a brief time]

The legal employers will use any excuse in the book to pay educated workers slave wages. I suspect they will still be using the 2008 economy, followed by the 2020 pandemic economy as their favorite excuse come 2050. "Well, you know just as soon as we start recovering, we get hit again. We just can't recover fast enough…" Yeah try being a worker for you guys instead of actually living off the profit sharing!

Of course not everyone is the same. You may find a group of people who seem as though they value your contributions. If you believe that is true, keep drinking the Kool-Aid and party on. But remember, you are most likely going to top out at under $75k in your position. Those rare birds who only work and do nothing else, may sacrifice everything precious to clear $100k. And when deals go down, you are going to be the only one sitting at the table who doesn't make millions from the deal. You can clean up the mess and go home to a microwave dinner. The lawyers will go run up a $10,000.00 strip club bill and not even blink.

When it comes down to your annual review (if you even get one, I might add), it will be a group of partners acting out their God Complex sitting around a table talking about you without any input from you whatsoever. These strangers who do not care about you will sit around and decide what you are worth. They might even throw some scraps at you. As a good dog, you will lap it up enthusiastically and gratefully thank them for their generosity this year.

If this is going to bother you, you have to find another way.

The following pages contain exhibits that I have used to demonstrate what your life as a paralegal could be. These are all absolutely real emails that I have modified in name and subject only. I just wish I could have known all this stuff before I went down this path. Heed my warnings. Choose wisely.

EXHIBIT 1

DECODING THE JOB ADVERTISEMENT

The first rule of business: If you ever see a job description or an advertisement that reads anything like this, run!

Seeking self-motivated person who loves to be helpful to manage a busy desk. Must be able to multi-task and work well with all types of people. Flexible hours, no overtime.

Let me decode this for you. Self-motivated and helpful means they want you to be a gunner, who will get fired up about the job and take on all kinds of extra responsibilities without asking for additional compensation. The ability to multi-task means someone is going to give you tasks and then constantly run in and out of your office all day changing their mind about the assignment they gave you, essentially making your entire job completely ineffective (not to mention unbearably frustrating). "All types of people" means that someone over there is either completely insane, a complete bitch, or a combination of the two (see below email for example of this). "Flexible hours, no overtime" means that YOU must be available to work late or on the weekends at a moment's notice, and that you will not be paid overtime "since you are on salary."

SECRETARY /PARALEGAL Busy law firm seeks experienced Secretary/Paralegal with verifiable attendance history and work ethic. PI/WC experience preferred. Strong references required. Excellent opportunity to trade your high heels for sandals!

You don't even need me to discuss this one, right? In case you are wondering yes, this is a real job that was advertised as late as April 6, 2014. Just know that if you take this job you are going to be constantly sexually harassed, and it is completely clear that your boss does not intend to ever treat you like the professional you are. One of his top concerns is that he just finds someone who will show up everyday!

> *Our firm is currently searching for a Personal Injury Case Manager specialist to help our personal injury practice. PLEASE NOTE: We are looking for someone with experience either part time or full time but experience with Personal Injury/Auto Accident Law is a requirement. MUST BE energetic, able to multi-task to the point of stopping in the middle of a task, to work on another and jump RIGHT BACK into the previous task. We are a very energetic firm that requires full attention, patience, drive and the complete ability to do several jobs for 2-3 people at once.*
>
> *The ideal candidate will possess the following attributes:*
>
> *1) Personal Injury Law knowledge and experience;*
> *2) Organizational skills; ability to multi-task;*
> *3) Self-motivated;*
> *4) Has a desire to have autonomy;*
> *5) Strong communication skills; Ability to talk to clients and reassure them as well; Ability to talk to other Attorneys and Adjusters about our clients' cases.*
> *6) Outgoing BUT focused!*
>
> *We need someone who is passionate, experienced and looking to help us grow.*

I am not kidding you when I say that I see this advertisement run about every three months. Anyone who thinks this is a proper way to run a business is just spinning his wheels running it into the ground. The most effective way to be a paralegal is to get all of your task assignments in the morning and then be able to go to your quiet office and actually work the tasks. No one needs a crazy boss running in and out of the office spouting out every different possible way we could do a task. You want a decisive boss who will just talk to you when he has decided what he wants you to do. Multi-tasking is a myth. Studies have shown that it is impossible to focus on two language-based tasks at once (sorry, there is no such thing as reading and comprehending an email and having an effective phone conversation simultaneously).

Example of Crazy/Bitchy Co-Worker, and How New Girl Handles Her (all too common in the law office)

From: New Girl
To: Experienced Paralegal
Subject: Singapore

Do you remember how to do this?

From: Experienced Paralegal
To: New Girl
Subject: RE: Singapore

No, I am sorry I do not. When I get done answering two subpoenas, calling and following up on a filing, finishing billing, preparing a notice of deposition, writing two letters to clients, and completing a Trademark filing I will look into it. Just a side note: If you feel like your load is getting too heavy, I would speak to A. Big Shot Attorney.

From: New Girl
To: Experienced Paralegal
Subject: RE: Singapore

A simple "I can help you later" would have sufficed. We are all busy around here, and we all have deadlines to meet. Yes, even me now.

Every time you have asked me for something I have done my best to help you with it, and have been glad that I could do it. I have always tried to be courteous to you and would appreciate the same consideration. I was not asking you to do this, I was just inquiring as to whether you had your notes readily available from the meeting we had with Baby Lawyer pertaining to this matter.

I am sorry if you are having a bad day, but I don't feel as though your comments towards me were warranted at all.

RUN LIKE HELL if you see a job description that is anything remotely like what I told you about in the above example! Crazy co-workers can be handled, but the job description is not going to change. You cannot accept work with the expectation that you are going to change how the lawyers work. They want to do what they do, and will want you to adapt and change to fit them. Know this going in, and prepare yourself mentally to do this if you want to stay employed.

EXHIBIT 2

WORKING WITH ASSOCIATES (a/k/a WHAT'S THAT SMELL?)

Some of the associates you work for will be precious. If they are fresh out of school, they will not know anything, and the best ones will come to you and readily admit it. These people, you can help. Especially watch out for the males. They tend to skip bathing and their offices and persons generally tend to take on a certain cheese or old gym sock smell. Sometimes it is because they forget to throw their food away (as evidenced below):

From: Legal Intern
To: Minion Paralegals
Subject: RE: New Associate

Justin is afraid to tell Administrator, but he thinks he left some food in his desk from over the summer.

Some associates are fun to play with. They don't know if you are serious or not. See below email re the firm policy on sharing hotel rooms. The poor guy didn't know if I was serious or not. He never responded back to me.

From: Baby Lawyer
To: Senior Paralegal
Subject: Bartow v. Oslo

We are good. Please don't do reservations under one name anymore. Almost had to wait for The Conquistador to get here.

From: Senior Paralegal
To: Baby Lawyer
Subject: Re: Bartow v. Oslo

You mean they gave you two rooms? Oh no. There's going to be hell to pay for that one down the line, I'm sure.

Didn't you get that TPS Memo? The firm just enacted some new travel policy. Let me find it in my handy 4 inch thick employee manual. Boring bullshit rule, ya da ya da..... some such stipulation about vacation and not having too much fun EVER.....

Here it is: BS Section 571.22(a)(i): "Whenever two attorneys of the same gender (who are believed to be heterosexual) are traveling on a case, those two attorneys must share a hotel room to keep costs down. Alternatively, two rooms may be reserved IF the total cost of both rooms (including all parking, internet, and taxes) does not exceed $200.00. Please note that this rule applies to all cities in the world, and not just Bumblefuck, Iowa."

You guys were <u>totally</u> supposed to be in the same room. You're in trouble.

Other associates will just drive you crazy with their idiotic/incompetent assignments. Associate syndrome is very real, and very dangerous to your mental health.

Watch out for tasks like this:

From: New Associate
To: Minion Paralegal
Subject: Task

Can you call the Superior Court of Kings county and see what info you can get on the divorce proceedings of Jennifer and John Lopez?

From: Minion Paralegal
To: Other Minion Paralegals
Subject: FW: Task

Honestly, I do not know what the hell this means.

From: Minion Paralegal
To: Other Minion Paralegals (and Boyfriend)
Subject: RE: Task

I'm serious. This needs to be my last day. These people just drive me cussing crazy.

I'm obviously completely incapable of being of service. I'm about to just get in my car and call it. I hate this bullshit.

All I can think is "Well great. There is a lot of information I can find out in a divorce file. Does New Associate want me to call the clerk and have the clerk recite the juicy financial bits regarding income, assets, and debt? Does New Associate just want to know when the divorce petition was filed and if it is still pending? Or, is this New Associate's veiled way of trying to get me to spend $200 on a courier to go out there and bring back a copy of the entire file, so he can yell at me for spending too much money on a courier and copy fees?"

Since I'm not a mind reader, I can't predict with any accuracy what it is EXACTLY that New Associate wants to know. And I just don't have the fight in me to jack around with these monkeys anymore. Why do I have to fight to be of service? Why can't the lawyer just tell me what they want? I'm so sick and tired of fighting what are supposed to be my own people. I'm serious. I can't do it, not even for one more CUSSING HOUR.

This is about to be the proverbial straw, people. New Associate is about to be the straw.

<u>Also, be on guard for fun with exhibits and filing motions as evidenced below:</u>

From: Minion Paralegal
To: Boyfriend
Subject: FW: motion

This is what I'm expected to sort out. Drafts that have been circulating with four different lawyers commenting on it. Some emails, going through to each other and not even copying me.

Exhibits that are identified as "that letter, you know, the one that is good for us. Find that letter that is good for us and mark it as Exhibit A."

I go out in the world and I'm so happy and excited about being alive.

And then I come in here and I want to just blow my cussing brains out.

From: Minion Paralegal
To: New Associate
Subject: Motion Under Seal
Importance: High

A. Big Shot Attorney wants the response and/or exhibits filed under seal. Under federal rules you have to file a motion requesting that the exhibits be filed under seal. We just can't file something under seal without making the appropriate motion with the Court. Can you please prepare that motion?

From: New Associate
To: Minion Paralegal
Subject: RE: Motion Under Seal

Do we not have one on file already that you can work with? It should be pretty basic. I'm trying to finish our response...

From: Minion Paralegal
To: Other Minion Paralegals
Subject: FW: Motion Under Seal

Example of what we discussed this morning. A. Big Shot Attorney asked me to have New Associate prepare the motion. Oh well, I've got to put on my attorney hat and get this motion done. Too bad I don't even know what is confidential in the response and/or exhibits to even prepare it, but I can BULLSHIT like the rest of them. I don't mind doing my job, when others do their job. I am truly surrounded by assholes and idiots.

If you aren't careful with new associates, they can really get you and the clients into

a lot of trouble, as evidenced below:

On October 12, 20__, Minion Paralegal wrote to Cool Associate:

New Associate is sitting in a depo and asked me to call some nurse who is somehow involved in this case and ask her about signing off on a surgery. Then he wants me to advise the client's daughter whether or not to sign off on the guy's surgery. I absolutely will not be doing that. Ever. And further, I don't think it is something that ANY member of this firm should be doing. TF does he think is going to happen if something goes wrong in the surgery and the guy dies. Then the wife comes back and says "Well my attorney told me to sign off on this."

New associates will also do stupid and insulting things like attempting to reward

you with cookies and candies instead of money. See below:

From: Minion Paralegal
To: Cool Associate; Other Minion Paralegals
Subject: Jackass Associate / What Do you Want, a Cookie?

I can't believe I forgot to tell you this.

Last Friday, I got stuck here late because the Big Pharma Defendants decided to hand-deliver a MSJ at 5:05. So I got finished scanning everything in and emailing it out, and Jackass Associate walks out of his office with a box of girl scout cookies and is trying to reward me with this box of cussing cookies.

You have to remember that the baby lawyers are under tremendous pressure as well, though, which explains why every email they will send you is an "ASAP" request. It's really not their fault.

From: Baby Lawyer
To: Paralegal
Subject: ASAP Records Request

We need to request Jeff's medical records from the hospital, Dr. George, and Dr. Stephen. We also need to get records from Jeff's gastroenterologist, whose name I can't remember. This would all be for his colorectal cancer treatment which pre-dated the injury. Please send requests and get this information asap.

From: Paralegal
To: Other Minion Paralegals
Subject: FW: ASAP Records Request

Does he do anything that isn't ASAP?

From: Baby Lawyer
To: Paralegal
Subject: Who is Yelling

Was that Doug or Conquistador that just yelled fuck?

From: Paralegal
To: Baby Lawyer
Subject: Re: Who is Yelling

Doug

From: Baby Lawyer
To: Paralegal
Subject: Re: Who is Yelling

Good. That means I don't have to deal with it.

EXHIBIT 3

SORRY PAYROLL DIDN'T GO THROUGH, I WAS SKIING THE SWISS ALPS

The real story is A. Big Shot Attorney went on a fabulously luxe ski vacation and forgot all about us minions back at the ranch. He was supposed to authorize payroll, but of course was too busy living the high life to bother with the likes of us. The official version that we got from the Administrator is below, but word got out pretty quickly what was really going on.

From: Administrator
To: Minion Paralegals
Subject: Payroll Notice
Importance: High

Everyone,

There was a minor accounting error, as such, our payroll will not be direct deposited into our checking accounts tomorrow. Instead it will be deposited on Monday. If anyone needs a hand written check tomorrow rather than waiting for the direct deposit on Monday – **Please let me know by 4:30 this afternoon**, otherwise your check will be deposited via direct deposit on Monday.

EXHIBIT 4

WE TALKED ABOUT GIVING BONUSES. I ASSUMED THEY WENT THROUGH. SORRY ABOUT THAT.

The last big project I ever did, I wound up getting screwed out of a bonus. They admittedly approved my bonus and just never got around to paying me. I could never keep working for them after this.

Needless to say, the bonus NEVER came through, and it completely broke my heart and ruined my confidence in my superiors. It was a mistake I could never square in my mind (or in my heart). How could they forget about me when I had built my life around taking care of them? All various explanations as to why the bonus never came through were all found by me to be completely unacceptable. I knew from experience that people take care of the things that are important to them to take care of. Whatever the reason, none of them mattered to me after about three months of waiting. How could I stay in an organization that blatantly did not keep their word to me? The trust was gone. I could no longer follow them into hell when I couldn't believe a word they said.

EXHIBIT 5

THE 24 HOUR MOVE

I, along with another minion paralegal in our office, was once in charge of orchestrating an office move. Most people would probably be allowed to close for the day, or at least for a few hours on Friday afternoon, but not us. Oh, no. Not us. We began our move at 5:00 p.m. on Friday night, and did not finish until 7:30 a.m. Saturday morning. A. Big Shot Attorney and other Associates were nowhere to be seen throughout the entire move. Do you think we got paid overtime or got an additional day off work as compensation? C'mon! You know better than that by now, don't you? Instead, on Monday when we got in, A. Big Shot Attorney wanted to know why we had not gotten more of the files put away in the filing cabinets. It was our fault; we should have worked 48 hours straight, of course.

You will notice that I do not have an email reflecting this move. It was so upsetting and traumatizing to me that in order to stay employed I immediately deleted all evidence of the experience so I could keep going to my job and functioning. Sometimes, in order to survive, you have to momentarily forget.

EXHIBIT 6

HAULING WATER

This is to demonstrate how the trial paralegal is basically responsible for putting together the entire case for trial, yet still ends up having to do demeaning and dehumanizing tasks such as moving cars around, hauling water, and all sorts of other ridiculous crap. Attorneys can be very high maintenance, and they do not care who has to do what, as long as somebody is fetching the snacks and bringing them water. Just know this going in, and make sure you eat a big breakfast before trial to keep your energy up.

Email reflections about life at trial:

From: Minion Paralegal
To: Other Minion Paralegals
Subject: Seriously

Why can't people put their garbage in the trash? It makes me so mad having to clean up after 8-10 adults every single day. I just think it is so disgusting and disrespectful to the courtroom and to me. Gross! Assholes. They throw their trash under the table and chairs and I have to crawl on my knees to pick up garbage every damn day. I thought about having my parents come watch trial one day, but I quickly realized that I don't want them to see me this way. Picking up trash and playing fetch all day long. I want them to maintain the illusion that their daughter went to college to become something other than a servant. Taking care of an entire entourage is VERY HARD.

From: Minion Paralegal
To: Other Minion Paralegal
Subject: Now he

Just told me to make sure they have bags of Altoids. Guess I'm going to the store after court. Can these people do one single personal task for themselves?!

From: Minion Paralegal
To: Other Minion Paralegal
Subject: Water

Jackass Associate just made me pour him a glass of water. I'm sitting next to him at Counsel's table doing depo designations, and he goes "Can you pour me a glass of water?"

From: Minion Paralegal
To: Other Minion Paralegals
Subject: Being a Minion at Trial

Minion – do you have a stapler?

Minion – can I have some water?

Minion – can you get your hands on where the Defendant talks about that important issue? WHERE is that paper that is good for us?!?!

Minion – can you print those photos?

Minion – do you have any tissues?

Minion - can you go move my car? The parking meter is almost up.

Minion - seriously, keep those cold waters coming.

Minion - go pull the fire alarm so we can take a break.

During one huge trial, I had to get the other minions in the office to get a courier to deliver some special snacks to the courtroom (that A. Big Shot Attorney was never going to eat):

From: Minion Paralegal
To: Other Minion Paralegals
Subject: A. Big Shot Attorney needs protein bars - an assortment with almonds and natural ingredients ASAP he doesn't like the candy bars

EXHIBIT 7

A TALE OF MONUMENTAL EGOS

The best example I can give you is that one time our firm hired what can now only be referred to as a real life Conquistador as a partner. Boy, was that guy a comedy of errors. He was mostly nice to the paralegals, though, because we were the only ones who could not be mean to his face. He had a terminal case of Conquistador Syndrome, too. This means he liked to eat long lunches, take vacations, and just generally avoid doing any substantive work whatsoever. It is a good job if you can keep it! See emails below:

From: Minion Paralegal
Subject: The Day The Court of Appeals Judge Came For Lunch
To: Cool Associate

Today, I got introduced by The Conquistador to a Court of Appeals Judge in front of a room full of people as "and that's Minion Paralegal. She's the brains behind the operation." <u>Hilarious</u>! But hey, I do know where my car keys and cell phone are at least 85% of the time (unlike some Conquistadors around here). Probably. And I don't overly drool. [I do sometimes have a problem making my mouth on the first try when I am eating and drinking, so I could stand some improvement there, but I don't think The Conquistador even knows about this].

Then, I attended a business lunch where a bow tie demonstration was given. I could hardly believe my good luck. That demo alone bumped up my resume qualifications.

The afternoon was topped off by The judge's recitation of a case involving "some paradoctor person." A. Big Shot Attorney looked at me and said "did you think that was funny?" Everyone looked at me while I declared how funny the judge was. But I don't think I fully got the smirk off, so I don't know if they believed me. Sometimes I am not in the mood to play actress.

Also, my opposing force theory needs some work. This morning, I had been considering that when two such egos combined, they might cancel each other out. Wishful thinking. Obviously this is impossible. A review of Newton's laws will be undertaken after I have had my coffee in the morning. I'm sure there's one that says "When giant egos collide, much jackassery will ensue." Awesome day.

When they finally figured out how to get rid of the unproductive Conquistador, this was the official story that was given:

From: A. Big Shot Attorney
To: Minion Paralegals; All Associates
Cc: Other Big Shot Attorneys
Subject: Emails
Importance: High

As many of you know, The Conquistador is leaving the firm. We are parting amicably and we wish him the best. The transition will happen over the next few days and weeks.

Please do not copy The Conquistador on any firm related emails or case related emails. If there is a need to copy him on something, please get approval from the Big Shot Attorney working on that case.

Thanks.

Full disclosure would dictate that I do confess that there was a no-holds barred email version of the Conquistador's departure that I got a copy of. But that, ladies and gentlemen, is currently being stored in a secret vault. After all, my legal education taught me nothing if not the fact that it is always in a Paralegal's best interest to hold a few secrets back.

<u>On avoiding calls from The Conquistador:</u>

From: Minion Paralegal
To: Other Minion Paralegals
Subject: Jackass Associate told me to send this email

Apparently The Conquistador just called but no one wanted to talk to him, so nobody picked up the phone.

Jackass Associate didn't say we HAD to pick up The Conquistador's calls in the future, just that I needed to send this email.

DONE!

The Conquistador takes a leisurely lunch and then steals one of the staff member's grocery bags on his way home:

-----Original Message-----
From: Conquistador
To: Administrator
Subject: Administrator, please send to everyone

Corleone's, the restaurant that is a leisurely five minute walk from our office, now serves lunches. I had not been there before and decided to try it today. My lunch was superb: grilled mahi-mahi with a half dozen spears of fresh asparagus. The chef was flexible, as he was willing to substitute olive oil for butter in the sauce (a lemon-butter sauce). Each asparagus spear was of just the right diameter (which, of course, may mean only that it was what was available in the market today). More important, it was cooked to a perfect degree of doneness, as was the fish. The meal as described (without my alcohol bill) was $10 plus sales tax--less than I've been paying for a sandwich. Based admittedly on but one lunch, I recommend this restaurant that is the one most convenient to our offices. I asked for both lunch and dinner menus for you to see. They are at the reception desk.
--Conquistador

P. S. Different matter: I have found that the little bag of groceries I took home last evening from the 2nd floor refrigerator was not mine. (Among whatever else, It had a package of shredded cheddar cheese in it.) Will the rightful owner please contact me today? I won't be in the office for the next six weeks.

The below email is not even about The Conquistador, this is just a fun example of an opposing attorney being a huge jackass. They honestly cannot help themselves, in my opinion.

-----Original Message-----

From: Michael S. Munster Van Dick
To: Other Big Shot Attorneys; Minion Paralegals
Subject: RE: Depos

I am fine with those dates (BTW, I had given them to your Minion Paralegal first of last week to start this rolling again--- also, I go by Michael, not Mike).

From: Minion Paralegal
To: Other Minion Paralegals
Subject: FW: Depos

How about I just call you Asshole.

EXHIBIT 8

SEX, DRUGS, ROCK 'N ROLL aka I'M JUST A DIRTY OLD MAN

From time to time, you may come across some incriminating emails, or see some weird photos around the copier or in someone's office. You might come across a picture of a paralegal and her married boss in the back of a horse-drawn carriage while they are across the country somewhere, for instance. The best thing that you can do is act as if you did not see a thing. Make sure you save exact copies of whatever you saw and do not distribute them to anyone. Keep hard copies in a safe deposit box, and keep the digital files archived in your secret cloud software storage of your choosing. You never know when the evidence might come in handy for you, but resist the temptation to share it. In the law business, you never want anyone to know all of the cards you can play. Also, I believe it is best to save innocent families from the truth as much as possible. Usually, as a paralegal, the truth is not yours to tell. You can store it, index it, and mull it over, but some pieces of evidence have to just be known to you.

I personally will never forget my experience with a self-proclaimed "dirty old man" deep in the heart of one of America's small towns, at a firm where the partners still believe they are living in the firm's founding year. I was subjected to pantomimed sex acts in the hallway outside my boss's door in full view of several employees, but no one could stop it. Apparently, this is just how this place rolls and nobody cares. Once in the lobby, around Christmas, the dirty old man pulled out a novelty item (I later looked it up on Amazon) that was the size of a hand sanitizer with a label affixed that proclaimed "I love my Penis!" My response? "Well, isn't that something?" There was nothing to be gained by going to the

Managing Partner or the Firm Administrator. Not when I knew that they had already been copied on such little email nuggets as:

From: Firm Administrator
To: All Big Shot Attorneys
Subject: Website News

If you have any news for our website, please forward your blurb to me. Thanks.

From: Dirty Old Man
To: Firm Administrator; All Big Shot Attorneys
Cc: Minion Victim Paralegal
Subject: RE: Website News

Word has it that Big Titty Ninnie won the Halloween Wet Tee Shirt Contest at Hooters on Sat night.

From: Dirty Old Man
To: Firm Administrator; All Big Shot Attorneys
Cc: Minion Victim Paralegal
Subject: Super Lawyers Top List Lawyer

We know this list is bullshit but apparently John Q. Public does not so we ought to get a press release perhaps with a picture.

From: Managing Partner
To: Firm Administrator; All Big Shot Attorneys; Dirty Old Man
Cc: Minion Victim Paralegal
Subject: re: 20___ Super Lawyers Top List Lawyer

Someone needs to read the part about online enhancement and paying to have this on the electronic version. I am less concerned about the paper. I do not know if we need to spend that money or not.

From: Dirty Old Man
To: Firm Administrator; All Big Shot Attorneys
Cc: Minion Victim Paralegal
Subject: Re: 20___ Super Lawyers Top List Lawyer

The hell with the online enhancement, whatever that is. I am much more concerned with enhancing my tally whacker! I was thinking about the Business Page in the Sunday paper where they have head shots of people getting promotions, awards, etc. A little head never hurt anyone so I am told. I would love a "head" shot. I will be on Bourbon street tonight looking for enhancement. Notice that I said just looking. It is like going to the zoo. You can look but you can't pet the beavers.

Bear in mind that at the end of the year, this group of degenerates will sit around a table and discuss your life and make plans for your future (or your future elimination) without you ever having a hand in the process. This is the group who will assign your worth. Is that what you want for yourself?

EXHIBIT 9

I KNOW IT'S THE FRIDAY BEFORE CHRISTMAS, I JUST NEED YOU TO…

Truthfully, this effect is something that is more commonly caused by the Associates. It could be because you know what rolls downhill, or it could be jealousy. After all, even paralegals are allowed out of the office at Christmas.

From: Minion Paralegal
To: Other Minion Paralegals
Subject: We can't

Understand for the life of us why Jackass Associate has to live up to his name anytime a partner tells us we can get out of jail before 5.

He is notorious for inventing "emergency" tasks at the last minute.

His favorite thing to say to us is "this is a 1/2 work day - not a no work day."

Then I hear him on the phone yukking it up. Yuk, yuk, yuk.

So Merry Christmas.

EXHIBIT 10

WHILE YOU'RE ON VACATION, COULD YOU...

This is really sort of just beating the dead horse to get my point across. Do you have it yet? Your life will never be your own again. You will be on call, just as if you were a surgeon. The difference is that you will only be making about a quarter of a surgeon's salary. Govern yourself accordingly or make other career plans.

On December 22, 20___, Minion Paralegal wrote:

Jackass Associate asked me to work from home e-filing something in one of our cases the day after Christmas. I of course at the time told him sure. Tomorrow, I think I will tell him that sounds like something he can handle on his own. Or Other Associate or Other Newer Associate. I don't think that sounds like something I should be doing right now at all.

The icing on the cake of course was that the brief is almost ready, they just don't want to give it to the other side yet. Okay. Leave me out of it. You closed the office, but you want ME to work?! How is that okay?!?! Am I wrong!?!

On December 22, 20___, Other Minion Paralegal wrote:

U r not wrong. I'm not giving this firm anymore than my 8 hours a day and am looking for another job. I'm done giving without getting. Like u said actions speak louder than words. I think this most recent action speaks volumes. I really think a body is a body. Someone else can handle it.

On December 22, 20___, Minion Paralegal wrote:

The bottom line is they don't care one iota back about me like I cared about them. If the firm was a man, I would have broken up with him a long time ago.

Why in the hell would that son of a bitch think I should jackass around with him when the office is closed?!?!? The more I think about it, the angrier I get. I'm starting to think they really do want me to just quit. You can't hijack people's free time constantly and expect them to 1. Accept it. 2. Be happy with it. No. I can't stay late. I'm pretty sure my kid is having a Christmas program that I need to get to......
Do you know that mothercusser was in my office last Friday at 6:15 telling me how important it is that A. Big Shot Attorney has a nice quality of life. What?!?! Every person

wants quality of life. No one wants to work for 3 weeks straight on some random meaningless project until 11, not see their families, miss a relative dying alone in hospice, and then have their bosses hit them with the same bonus they gave the girl who has worked here for a couple months, or the girl who NEVER worked 3 days straight in a row her whole cussing life probably.

These people are a bunch of communist socialists. They don't reward hard work and loyalty. They punish it. They beat it until it is dead. How is this my life?!?!?!

From: Other Minion Paralegal
To: Minion Paralegal
Subject: Re: Day after Xmas

I'm so glad it is Friday and I only have to make it through today. I've been awake for over an hour with stomach issues over my worthlessness. Today A. Big Shot Attorney turned an interviewee away bc he didn't think she was ready for this job. She agreed and said she wasn't anywhere near ready to handle or even wanted to handle the job we were describing. Silly me. And I was sitting there thinking how its takes people who are really special to do this job and A. Big Shot Attorney sees that. What a fool I am.

EXHIBIT 11

YOU'RE A USELESS MORON BECAUSE YOU CAN'T READ MY MIND

I'm not kidding you. This is a real job expectation. They like to code it to "ability to anticipate needs." I actually once overheard A. Big Shot Attorney telling a New Associate that he was of no use to him if he couldn't anticipate his needs. For real. ESP is a job requirement in the legal field. Ask around. I assure you I am not putting you on. I still scratch my head over how miserably attorneys communicate. I honestly think they just don't care to communicate. In fact, they actually hate clarity, because they get paid more when a situation is as difficult as possible. I have news for you – everything will be as complicated and as difficult as they make it. Reality is often very far away from how attorneys like to paint it. Just know this.

From: Minion Paralegal
To: Other Minion Paralegals
Subject: A. Big Shot Attorney needs papers he lost emailed ASAP

He said one was used in the Richardson matter. He also said, "I had it yesterday." To which I said: "I don't know what you did with your document."

From: Minion Paralegal
To: Other Minion Paralegal
Subject: Also

Really love when they ask me for things that don't exist, and deny remembering what they told me to do.

EXHIBIT 12

AN ASSORTMENT OF RPP

"RPP" means Rich People Problems. You know you have them if you have to get your paralegal to make a spreadsheet of your properties that need to be refinanced. Your boss is living on a different planet than you are. After trial, they can afford to jet off at the drop of a hat to wherever they want. You are too tired to plan a weekend getaway to a city two hours away. And besides, you can't afford to pay last minute airfare costs! Your boss will also have problems such as not being able to fit all the people he wants into his private suite to watch a professional sports team. You will have to keep a list and update it when people piss him off so you can suggest cuts. These people you work for are not like you. Their problems include which European city they will visit this summer so they can purchase period furniture for their vacation home(s). Their wives are on waiting lists to buy handbags and cars. It's another world entirely. It can sometimes be very irritating to watch. You will want to scream at them: "I was at the grocery store last night trying to figure out what the cheapest meat is!" They don't get it. Once, A. Big Shot Attorney overheard me complaining about my commute and asked me why I didn't just buy a townhouse in the city. Gosh, I sure wish I was smart enough to think about that all on my very own! Also, be forewarned: They know they are nothing like you. When speaking among themselves, they will refer to all other non-attorneys as "regular people." The young female lawyers live in fear of being mistaken as "staff" by clients and visitors in the office.

From: Minion Paralegal
To: Other Minion Paralegal
Subject: RE: Rich People Problems

Maybe I should ask genius over here why he doesn't just send someone from his local firm to cover this depo if he's so worried about him's missing him's nap.

Gosh, you would think this firm didn't have 65 other attorneys in their satellite office alone. Poor A. Big Shot Attorney - hims has to travel to every fact deposition that is taken, and hims has a hard life! Truth be told, ever since Delta lost his blanket five years ago, he hasn't fully recovered. I mean, he still has his binkie, but he can't snuggle with that. He is most comforted when he is swaddled in a nice soft blanket, not sucking on a piece of plastic.

His paralegal has made several attempts to replace the missing blanket, but hasn't been able to, as the particular wool was farmed out of a ranch in Australia, that closed back in the 1950's, not too long after A. Big Shot Attorney's mother first purchased the blanket.

The closest she has ever come was a few months ago, when she found a ranch in a remote (ha!) part of Tibet that actually wove blankets from children's hair. The texture was good, but ultimately it didn't work out because as we all know, A. Big Shot Attorney prefers blondes.

From: Minion Paralegal
Sent: xxxx
To: Cool Associate
Subject: RE: Life Sucks

If I hear one more dumbass question I am going to lose my mind and end up getting fired. No, I don't know why your phone/computer/security alarm at your house/pool heater won't turn on. I don't know where you parked your car or if it will get towed. I don't know why your shoes won't stay tied. And no, I don't know where your pen is. I also don't know the contents of your briefcase, who is currently renting your vacation property, or everyone in the world who tried to call you/email you today. I know, I don't know shit. I am completely useless to everyone. Maybe I should have stayed home today. Sometimes I just don't feel like playing, you know. Sometimes I just can't believe this is my life.

EXHIBIT 13

I'M STANDING AT THE TICKET COUNTER AT DELTA. CAN YOU CALL AND RESCHEDULE MY FLIGHT?

Basically, they are completely helpless and they will suck your will to live right out of you, as evidenced below:

From: Minion Paralegal
To: Other Minion Paralegal
Subject: I swear to GOD!

All I have been doing in this mothercusser is playing fetch with Jackass Associate. Can you print this? Can you bring me that?

I'm not a puppy. I think.

Wednesday night he called me at 5:15 because he was at the gate in Detroit. His flight had been cancelled. I'm like, why are you calling me? I'm not Delta. YOU'RE AT THE GATE. TALK TO THE GATE AGENT.

Earlier today, he interrupted me from the client photo demonstrative exhibit I was organizing for trial to tell me to create a signature sheet and Certificate of Service for a motion [that he is *still* at this very moment trying to get finalized for a courier who is sitting in the lobby to pick up, mind you] because they were all going to leave and go to a game together. I took the time to do it and walked it back to his office. Upon my arrival with said document, he informs me that he no longer needs it, he's staying. I said, "So everything you just had me do is worthless." To which the Conquistador replied: "But we appreciate your worthlessness."

Last night we had a storm up here. It took me 2.10 hours to get home. I'm becoming increasingly convinced that I'm dead, and this is hell.

Are we dead?

From: Other Minion Paralegal
To: Minion Paralegal
Subject: RE: I swear to GOD!

OMG, I swear I am having the same kind of day/week! You don't even know. I was JUST literally thinking on my drive in this morning that I must have died and gone to hell because that is what my life feels like right now.

I am the ONLY one in this office this week (except for the few hours A. Big Shot Attorney graced me with his presence on Monday and late yesterday) and I don't know what is worse ... Doing every single damn thing by myself for the entire office with no instruction or response from the managing partner OR doing every little thing he commands while someone is standing over my shoulder barking "open this," "print that," "scroll up," "scroll down," "rotate that" ... REALLY???

I truly feel like a crazy person most days and I just keep telling myself "be thankful you're employed, be thankful you're employed."

From: Minion Paralegal
To: Other Minion Paralegal
Subject: RE: I swear to GOD!

I do too know. I know everyone thinks I'm crazy, but I swear to God I didn't start out that way! The legal field has done it to me. My boyfriend says he can see how I've changed since I started working for lawyers.

From: Other Minion Paralegal
To: Minion Paralegal
Subject: RE: I swear to GOD!

I have aged 10 years in the past 2 and I'm serious about that. I'm not doing this to myself for the rest of my life. Like my Dad says, "Lawyers are vampires. They will suck you dry until there's not a drop left then they'll move on to the next victim." So true. I have been doing this for well over a decade and it is the same thing everywhere I go. I WILL be finding myself a new career eventually. I got offered a killer job the other week and I passed on it because I am so tired from this one that I can't imagine having the energy to learn a new one right now. Ugh. I always hear around here that we're supposed to hang in there because things will get better. They never will. They'll just lose us and start over with someone new who they'll say the same thing to.

From: Minion Paralegal
To: Other Minion Paralegal
Subject: RE: I swear to GOD!

You're killing me right now. Seriously. I can't tell you how often I have said those words about aging. And I know it is a cop-out, but I blame my recent 20 lb. weight gain on being stressed out from this job. I mean, I know I should get home at 7:00 and exercise, but it hardly ever happens. Taking care of myself is such a fight.

Your father and I agree on the vampire comment too.

It is so sad to see our passions and dreams die because we've sunk into this paralysis survival state where all we can think of is eat, sleep, drive, and just take care of basic needs. The other night I came home, and I was like, I can't even concentrate on watching tv. I just want to sit quietly. I sat in my living room and stared at the wall for a good thirty minutes. I was catatonic.

Really scary.

From: Other Minion Paralegal
To: Minion Paralegal
Subject: RE: I swear to GOD!

I hear you! We NEED balance in our lives. Please find a way to enjoy your weekend. It is sad that we have to get hammered to forget about work but that is probably what I'll be doing for the next couple days!

Below is another email string that a friend of mine from another firm shared with me. What is so frightening and enlightening is how these other two women across the country at a whole other law firm are discussing the very same phenomenon about getting used up and bled dry. It is enough to have me convinced that this goes on everywhere, and that just changing your job is not going to make anything better whatsoever. You will just be getting sucked up by a new team of attorneys. The game never changes, only the players change.

From: Legal Secretary
To: Paralegal
Subject: Other Paralegal just quit with NO notice....

AAAAAAAAAAAAAAAAAAAHHHHHHHHHHHHHHHHHHHHHHHHHHHHHHH HHHHH!

From: Paralegal
To: Legal Secretary
Subject: RE: Other Paralegal just quit with NO notice....

Uhm, WOW. I mean, not surprised she quit, but definitely surprised that she did without notice. I mean was there an event? And she was just like, I'm done, and walked out? How's everything else?

From: Legal Secretary
To: Paralegal
Subject: RE: Other Paralegal just quit with NO notice....

She just said she couldn't handle the pressure anymore. She just left a letter in our Big Shot Attorney's chair on Friday. WTF?!

We are so busy we have to have another paralegal. Our Big Shot Attorney asked me this morning to take the job.

From: Paralegal
To: Legal Secretary
Subject: RE: Other Paralegal just quit with NO notice....

My advice would be no. Once you're in it you're roped in worse than you are now. But it's up to you of course! But I'd ask for a HELL of a lot more $$$$$$. That is really shocking though that she just left a letter too. What was the reaction?

From: Legal Secretary
To: Paralegal
Subject: RE: Other Paralegal just quit with NO notice....

That's the catch. Our Big Shot Attorney said it wouldn't be much more $$$$, and I just don't know that I am willing to sacrifice my life for a couple of thousand dollars. I am thinking that is all I would be offered.

They are surprised and disappointed, but nothing they can do about it.

From: Paralegal
To: Legal Secretary
Subject: RE: Other Paralegal just quit with NO notice....

I'm gonna tell you right now, if they don't give you a pay increase that you feel you deserve, DON'T DO IT! I speak from experience it is NOT WORTH IT! (and I know you know that too) Especially since you are newly married and I know you're wanting to start a family. That added stress will not help any of that at all! There is a reason that they cannot keep paralegals there, just saying. I always kept thinking it would get better and I would be better treated, appreciated and paid and it never happened.

From: Legal Secretary
To: Paralegal
Subject: RE: Other Paralegal just quit with NO notice....

No, you are totally right. I told Our Big Shot Attorney I have to talk with my husband, but I think I already know I am not going to do it.

From: Paralegal
To: Legal Secretary
Subject: RE: Other Paralegal just quit with NO notice....

I know it's hard not to because it's like "Well there isn't much difference...", but that's the problem. It's a lot more work, a lot more responsibility, traveling, etc. And I think since you want to start a family...that added stress will just make it that much more difficult and could affect you not just mentally, but also physically. I mean if they only offer a couple thousand more, in all honesty, you won't even notice a difference on your pay check....and what's the freaking point of that!

EXHIBIT 14

YOU KNOW THAT CONFERENCE I DIDN'T TELL YOU I WAS ATTENDING? WHERE AM I STAYING?

Some attorneys like to pretend that they told you to do something, and then get mad when you neglected to do what they failed to ask you in the first place. Be prepared for this phenomenon. The best way you can guard against this is to be extremely proactive with looking ahead on the calendar to determine upcoming events that might require registering for a seminar, traveling to a deposition, and booking travel arrangements. This is one of those times where ignorance of the law is no excuse. You will get busted for not knowing. I know, I know. It just isn't fair.

EXHIBIT 15

IT'S 11:45 P.M. – I NEED YOU TO RESPOND TO THIS URGENT EMAIL.

The urgent email will usually be something along the lines of a forgotten password. They never know their user names and passwords. They would rather just email you late at night so you can look it up and tell them. Why would they spend a few seconds looking for something when they could just ask you? You will probably want to say: "Look, I don't have the keys to your bitcoin wallet, okay? I don't know what your password is. Get it together. How do you even find your way to the office every day?"

If you want to keep your job, you are just going to have to deal with it like a good servant.

EXHIBIT 16

DON'T F*** IT UP

Here is where the paralegal is given responsibilities beyond the average five-year associate at a big firm and basically told "Good luck. Don't f*** it up." Sometimes it is funny, and you can think of it as a sort of hazing exercise to separate the men from the boys. Other times it is sheer insanity, and you cannot think about it too much or the pressure will get to you. You do not want to be the paralegal who has to go to the hospital because of heart palpitations. Just bootstrap it and remember – "Don't f*** it up."

Just another day in court:

From: Minion Paralegal
To: Other Minion Paralegals
Subject: Re: Invoices

Thanks. Not even 9 and I already could vomit. If they would just tell me what they need, I could have it for them. But I'm the dumbass. Not because they don't review exhibits. The problem is clearly me.

Dealing with the stress of trying to get ready for trial:

From: Minion Paralegal
To: Other Minion Paralegal
Subject: Will they ever

Just leave you the hell alone so you can concentrate on getting your trial ready?!?!?!?!!?

From: Other Minion Paralegal
To: Minion Paralegal
Subject: RE: Will they ever

NO WAY. I thought I was doing really good and then the sky fell out yesterday. I wanted to leave this Wed. and get MYSELF together, but who knows now. Somehow these guys have got to get more organized so that I don't have a stroke every time I have to prepare and go to trial. I'm a maniac!

From: Minion Paralegal
To: Other Minion Paralegal
Subject: RE: Will they ever

Me too. I thought I was going to have a heart attack yesterday. During trial prep, I am constantly "On Call," like a doctor or a nurse and it is really hard on me and my family (as you can attest to). Anyway, to sum up as quickly as possible, X had their portion of the PTO to me as agreed, early enough to finalize it and get the courier over here. Then, The Conquistador starts deciding that he wants to make revisions to it at 4:15. I send it back to opposing counsel and she calls me immediately. "What?! Now, I have to get this circulated again to my people." Then she's like, "I'm just going to call the court. We're not going to make our deadline. We're having technical problems with our exhibit list anyway."

It doesn't have to be so crazy. I went home yesterday at 6:50, feeling like someone had been beating the life out of me for the last 10 hours. I knew yesterday was going to be hard because it was a deadline day. But I pumped myself up for it by telling myself – "this is all going to be over with by 4:00 because they will have to get you everything by then for the courier to make it to the courthouse." Little did I know. I was chained here until they quit feeling like engaging in general jackassery.

I mostly can't figure out what my job is. In my head I think it is TO BE A TRIAL PARALEGAL. But then I find myself being the secretary, the scheduler, the travel agent, etc. It is just really hard work.

Bottom line, we need to talk about how to make our job easier so we don't go crazy. No one likes being jacked around.

From: Other Minion Paralegal
To: Minion Paralegal
Subject: RE: Will they ever

I'M SO WITH YOU ON THIS YOU JUST DON'T EVEN KNOW. "JACKED AROUND" THAT IS TRULY HOW I FEEL RIGHT NOW. JACKED AROUND, JACKED OFF, JACKED OVER, CUSSING JACKED AND MOST OF ALL, A BLEEPING JACK ASS!

What happens when trial attorneys finally sit down and look at their case:

From: Other Minion Paralegal
To: Minion Paralegal
Subject: What the Hell?

Four days before trial, my attorneys and xxxx's attorneys must have decided to FINALLY LOOK at the case and all of a sudden I have a list a mile long of emergency tasks to do. Stuff that each side should have decided to do months ago.

Oh by the way I need to do the projects "as quickly as possible" so my boss can decide if, after looking at it, he EVEN WANTS TO USE IT IN COURT. Um?

EXHIBIT 17

WHATEVER IT TAKES, MAKE IT HAPPEN

While the mission is not always clear, it is extremely important that you be able to move heaven and earth. Even if it does not make sense to you, just move, move, move!

From: Minion Paralegal
To: Other Minion Paralegals
Subject: I have to get the hell out of here

From: Other Minion Paralegal
Sent: xxxx
To: Minion Paralegal
Subject: RE: I have to get the hell out of here

I know the feeling. Yesterday I threw up in my trash can from 100% pure stressed the hell-outedness and then cried. This place will kill a bitch!

On running for the sake of running:

From: Minion Paralegal
To: Big Shot Attorneys and Jackass Associate
Subject: Pedometer

I wore a pedometer today. You guys ran me around today for 4.20 miles. Thanks for the exercise I guess.

EXHIBIT 18

HI. I'M IN BERMUDA. OUR INSURANCE EXPIRES TODAY. MAKE IT MAGIC!

This is just one email example of being completely disconnected from reality and their law practice.

From: Other Minion Paralegal
To: Minion Paralegal
Subject: RE: Liability Insurance

Our damn professional liability insurance was about to expire today and A. Big Shot Attorney didn't think to mention that to me when he left a huge stack of insurance documents on my chair last night with scribbles here and there and no instructions to say "do this today or we're screwed!"

EXHIBIT 19

IT'S 4:00 ON THE FRIDAY BEFORE LABOR DAY. SURPRISE! YOU CAN LEAVE EARLY. OH, AND THE OFFICE WILL BE CLOSED ON MONDAY (a/k/a MY TIME & MONEY ARE VALUABLE, BUT YOURS AREN'T)

TIME

There are many and varied areas where attorneys will completely disrespect you. One of those topics is your time. They do not care about you wasting your own personal time in the pursuit of furthering their agendas. Paralegals would like to have a life outside the office. When there is not a trial going on, or a real deadline to meet, we want to cook dinner with our family and talk to our kids. We work to live, not live to work. This is probably one of the main reasons the paralegal stayed out of law school. When it becomes routine to stay late into the night and come in on weekends without getting paid overtime, that is a major problem. What employee would find that motivating?

In fact, the lawyers want you to spend as much time as you can on things that are important to their own agendas. See for yourself:

From: Minion Paralegal
To: Other Minion Paralegals
Subject: Tired

I'm really tired of getting my personal time hijacked and having to work late with no notice for no real reason except the lawyer didn't feel like working until now.

From: Minion Paralegal
To: Other Minion Paralegal
Subject: What is the firm policy on paying for meals when forcing employees to work late?

From: Other Minion Paralegal
To: Minion Paralegal
Subject: RE: What is the firm policy on paying for meals when forcing employees to work late?

There isn't any "policy" on that issue, but if I'm working after hours (or even during lunch) because it is REQUIRED AND NECESSARY to complete an assignment on time (usually trial time or trial prep) I would charge my meal to the case. It sounds like whatever it is you are doing is "out of the ordinary" and I consider that to be firm time and firm meal. You can always ask A. Big Shot Attorney. If it is from an atty other than A. Big Shot Attorney he may get on someone about keeping you late and through dinner and he may fix that situation for you.

From: Minion Paralegal
To: Other Minion Paralegal
Subject: RE: What is the firm policy on paying for meals when forcing employees to work late?

I tell you, everyone is just pissing me off to no end lately.

Friday night, it WAS A. BIG SHOT ATTORNEY!!! I had to stay here until 6:40 helping him with an expert disclosure because he did not get back from his drinking lunch until 4:45.

Then Monday, the guys totally screwed Mallory, and I stayed a little later (5:30 helping her, but had to bail bc I've been sick and was seriously going to drop if I didn't get the hell out of here).

Then, Jackass Associate just walks into my office and tells me he's going to be holding me hostage here tonight until some uncertain time because other Big Shot wants something e-filed with the Court of Appeals TONIGHT (our deadline isn't even until after Christmas), and Jackass Associate and Nice Associate are still revising it. Well, Jackass Associate, file it yourself. Or email it to me and let me do it from home at 7:00.

They just have no respect for me as a HUMAN BEING ANYMORE. They think nothing of completely ruining my night. It just pisses me off and makes me feel like I have no control over my life. That I exist at the pleasure of the firm.

I just want to come in here at 8:30 and WORK and leave on time so that I have 3-4 hours to cook something healthy, exercise, and settle down and rest for the next day. YOU KNOW, HAVE ENOUGH TIME TO TAKE CARE OF MYSELF SO I CAN KEEP COMING HERE EVERYDAY HELPING THESE PEOPLE MAKE MONEY. I swear to God, they think I'm a robot who powers down and goes into the closet in the back until it's time to work the next morning. They don't think I'm an actual human who needs anything.

From: Other Minion Paralegal
To: Minion Paralegal
Subject: RE: What is the firm policy on paying for meals when forcing employees to work late?

They do the same thing here. More so to Lisa than to me. These guys know I get here early, I have a long ride home and NOT to give me something at 3PM to get out. I have a family (and even if I didn't) I have AA, my psychiatrist, acupuncturist, my bipolar disorder support group, overeaters anonymous, etc., that I have to get to every single night of the week. So don't give me shit at the last minute. Seems lately everything is last minute. And as the days trickle by I feel EXTREMLY disrespected. I've worked my ass off this year covering for paralegals who suck or aren't here and it is 6 days before Christmas and I don't have money to buy anything for my kids. I'm sick about it. I feel disrespected that they've waited so long to give a bonus and now due to the extremely late date, I'm wondering if I'm even going to get one. How can people who "care" treat us like that? You know it is to the point that I'm not even pissed about this stuff anymore, I'm more hurt. I feel that there is a huge "sign" dangling around my head telling me where I stand and I just don't want to read the thing.

From: Minion Paralegal
To: Other Minion Paralegal
Subject: RE: What is the firm policy on paying for meals when forcing employees to work late?

I know. You are speaking my language. Mallory is much more of an optimist than I am.

They will say all the right things to you sometimes. They will even sing your praise. But actions speak louder than words. Or they should. I can't pay my bills with "You rock," or a cupcake. I'm just really unhappy lately, and I wish I wasn't. I wish I was still in love with the firm. But the firm is treating me like an asshole!

From: Minion Paralegal
To: Other Minion Paralegals
Subject: RE: Phones

I experienced Associate Failure to Plan Syndrome Last Night. I stayed until 7:30 doing trial prep stuff w/A. Big Shot Attorney (which is to be expected, but STILL SUCKS), but I also had a deadline getting discovery out. Clueless Associate came to me at 4:30 and Other Minion Paralegal can tell you more about it, bc she got stuck here too until about 7:15 or so fixing that mess. I just can't keep getting hijacked like this without being paid overtime. Both of us drive an hour plus home at night, and then can't wind down until after midnight. Up by 6:00 to get ready for work and do it all over again. It just is too much extra time that we are expected to continually give. (As I know you know). I want to work hard, but more than that even, I want to work smart and be efficient. And if I have to stay late, then I think it is more than fair to be compensated. My time is valuable to me. And it just makes me a better employee if I have my personal time to take care of myself – eat well, exercise, maintain and nurture relationships, etc. All of these things are an important and critical part of a balanced life. I can't be chained here every day wondering when they are going to let me out.

From: Minion Paralegal
To: Cool Associate
Subject: Re: xxxx - deposition notices -

Thank you for the encouragement. I don't know how I did it, they make me so crazy! Just constant jackassing around at the last minute. Basically, they think I'm their personal assistant, not a paralegal. What they need is a monkey to press print, and a dog to fetch them things. They've just 5 seconds ago pulled some crazy stunt on me about physically going to pick up a key from the housekeeper and going to get a copy made and then dropping one off at A. Big Shot Attorney's hotel. Real crazy type situation that I shouldn't be dealing with on the FRIDAY NIGHT BEFORE TRIAL. Just a whole list of diva crap like this that is extremely tiresome. Never again. I haven't said anything to any of the partners bc I know now isn't the time, but we're going to have a sit down when this is over and decide what my job is, because I have no clue what the hell is expected of me anymore. It really just is flat out ridiculous for them to be running me around at all hours for no real reason, except that they didn't feel like thinking about anyone but themselves. My time is just as valuable as theirs.

From: Minion
To: Other Minions
Subject: FW: Fax

A. Big Shot Attorney tells us around 10:00 a.m. that the office is closing at 12:00. At 11:57, Jackass Associate decides he needs to send this letter out. Typical. I yelled at him a little bit. He knows I'm trying to get out of town right now. This really pisses me off. He is famous for this. He can't stand for anyone to go out of town EVER.

Why in the world would anyone want to get their work done and leave early?!

From: Minion, on Behalf of A. Big Shot Attorney
To: Firm
Subject: Holiday Schedule

Merry Christmas! The firm will be closed Monday, December 24 – Wednesday, December 26. For the New Year the firm will be closed on Tuesday, January 1.

Hope everyone has a wonderful holiday! Go wherever it is you people go! *[Note - The guy is saying go power down in your rat holes until I call you back in here].*

Nothing like three business days notice for people to purchase flights to go back home for Christmas! Thanks for the notice A. Big Shot Attorney! You are so generous and thoughtful, I'm so glad I work here. Now I can call my mother and tell her I wished I had known three weeks ago when airfare was still under $1,000! But thanks to you, I can sit around in my sad apartment and eat frozen pizza. Awesome! Hey, it beats being at work, I guess.

From: A. Big Shot Attorney
Sent: xxxx
To: All Minions
Cc: Jackass Associate; Cool Associate
Subject: Hearing on Monday

We need some binders for the hearing on Monday. We would like to give the court a notebook of all the cases where Big Pharma has failed to turn over requested documents. Can you help us tomorrow to put these together?

From: Cool Associate
To: Minion Paralegal
Subject: Hearing on Monday

Didn't they know about this hearing on Wednesday? They wait until SAT afternoon to tell you that they need notebooks?

MONEY

The following email is truly priceless. STAFF are spending entirely too much money on office supplies and records to prove the client's cases. This has got to be stopped! We're going to save a fortune if we just cut costs on paper and the clips we use! Brilliant, surely this strategy will keep us from going under!

From: A. Big Shot Attorney
To: Firm
Subject: Policies
Importance: High

We had a very productive partners meeting last week (from my private villa in the Caribbean). One thing that we have all concluded and need to change is that this firm spends way too much money. A lot of it is unnecessary. Here are some of the changes the partners would like to implement:

1. We order way too many records to prove our case. Just order the good ones. A partner must approve an "order all of the records" request.

2. We use too many services when ordering these medical records. For the most part, we should be able to get the necessary records ourselves. Please get approval from a partner if you feel it is necessary to get a record service involved. *(Mind you, this is ridiculous because the facility chooses to use an outside company to handle records requests, and there is nothing that anyone can do about it).*

3. We need to put a limit on what we spend with companies like Cioxx. I realize that many doctor's offices contract with this company but their charges are ridiculous. Please tell them that we will pay 5 cents per page for copies. Anything more must be approved by a partner. *(Again, completely ridiculous. There is actually a statute that governs how much the facility can charge per page, and there is nothing that anyone can do about it. The partners are completely out of touch with how the world actually works).*

4. We need to start tracking our photocopies and postage. We need to keep a spreadsheet next to the copier. When you make copies for a case put the date, case name and number of copies. Use a similar spreadsheet for postage.

There may be some more changes in the future but we believe this is a good start. We realize these changes could cause some aches and pains in the short term but we are trying to create a more efficient and cost effective practice. This will benefit everyone in the long run.

Thank you. Let's have a great year.

This email still makes me chuckle. I have never witnessed a staff member do anything other than economize when it comes to running cases and ordering office supplies. I have seen my co-workers use scrap paper instead of using expensive legal pads, make double-sided copies and recycle notebooks, and use the free pens and post-its that our vendors give us rather than spend the money ordering supplies. The partners are just clueless!

EXHIBIT 20

LET'S SCHEDULE A CALL / MEETING ON THAT

One of Jackass Associate's favorite activities in the whole wide world is to have his paralegal schedule phone calls and meetings for him. Then, when the time rolls around, he'll blow it off and make the paralegal call the person who has been waiting to apologize for <u>her</u> scheduling error and arrange a new time to chat or meet. This will happen at least three times as a rule before the call or meeting ever actually happens. It is completely unprofessional to cancel events because you just aren't in the mood anymore.

The funniest part about all of this is when the paralegal calls the client in order to set up a call for later. Inevitably, the client will respond with a perplexed: "You've got me on the phone now, what does he want? Can't he just talk to me now?" The paralegal then has to admit the ridiculousness of the situation. "I know, Mr. Client. It's true that we're talking right now. As fun as this is, wouldn't the fun just be turned up beyond belief if we took what we're doing right now and put it off until later? Doesn't it make more sense for employees of this firm to call you multiple times to accomplish one task?" It makes complete sense to me...

EXHIBIT 21

WE NEED TO... WHY DON'T WE... LET'S...

This refers to the way of passive aggressive speaking which is so completely spineless, it angers me beyond belief. By failing to assign specific tasks to one person, nothing gets done. There is also the other side of the spectrum, where the lawyer assigns the same task to three different people so two staff members are wasting time on a redundant task that has already been completed.

One day when the receptionist was out and everyone else was away from their desks preparing for an upcoming trial.......

From: Different Big Shot Attorney Weighs In on the Issue
To: A. Big Shot Attorney
Cc: Firm
Subject: Re: Anyone answering the phones?

I had three different lawyers tell me the phones just rang and rang and rang with no answer today.

"A. Big Shot Attorney" wrote:

I have had a referring lawyer who said he called in twice and no one answered. This obviously is a huge problem. We need to make sure that we are answering the phones during business hours.

Thank you.

A. Big Shot Attorney

From: A. Big Shot Attorney
To: All Minions
Cc: Jackass Associate
Subject: Office hours

So I'm sitting here at 8:27 locked out of the office and no one is here. Silly me, I thought I wouldn't need a key since we open at 8:30.

EXHIBIT 22

I KNOW IT'S THE 4TH OF JULY AND YOU'RE GETTING YOUR SON FROM THE ARMY BASE, BUT CAN YOU JUST...

From: Minion Paralegal
To: Other Minion Paralegal
Subject: You Won't Believe What this Asshole Did to us Today

Since the trial settled so late last night, no one made it back to the home office. Last night, A. Big Shot Attorney called Jennifer and said he couldn't get out on Delta at 9:30 p.m., but that he was going to keep trying. Jennifer told him she was going to drive to pick up her son from the army base (this is the first time he's had a weekend pass in 6 months).

At 6:30 am Jennifer is already halfway to the base. By the time she parks the car and looks at her phone, she's got a voicemail from A. Big Shot Attorney wanting to know what time she's leaving to head back home because he needs a ride after all.

Mind you he's at the airport already with a full fare 1st class ticket. There are about 8-10 daily flights back home mind you. But he can't JUST THIS ONE TIME take his hour commercial flight back home. Oh, no. That would be crazy. Why spend $1,000 on a commercial first class ticket when you could make your employee come back and personally pick him up and drive him to his door?!

He makes Jennifer drive back and get him, son in full army uniform no less. He was just sick of the airport and "couldn't do this anymore." Of course he couldn't rent a car and drive himself. Don't be ridiculous!

What an absolute piece of shit. Poor xxxx hasn't been off the army base in 6 months and really just wanted to go to the beach. I felt so bad for him. He's actually serving our country and instead of one day off in six months he had to deal with this entitled pompadour princess asshole. Typical. By the time Jennifer got him home there were only four more hours of daylight left.

EXHIBIT 23

BUT I WANT IT

This refers to the inevitable tantrum session you will have to witness and endure when your attorney wants something that you just can't give him. For instance, maybe another law firm referred a case to your firm. Picture your attorney preparing for a deposition and having a certain report in mind that he once saw somewhere. He will task you: "I need that report I saw one time. I know we have it. It should be in the file." You will spend the next three hours reviewing the entire case file and showing him every report you find. Nothing you show him will be the correct report. His reply to you will be: "But I want it." He cannot tell you what it even is, exactly, that he is looking for, or even who you might call to obtain a copy, or even the originating agency or person. He will just be mad that you are completely incapable of finding the mysterious report. There may be some chair throwing involved. Duck! [As an aside, I would like to point out to all A. Big Shot Attorneys that no one is intimidated or amused by the tantrums. The paralegals think you are a giant donkey, and they make up t-shirts to wear behind your back that make fun of you. They may even be so bold as to bring those cleverly-phrased shirts out on casual Friday. You will have no idea they are even about you because you are so self-involved].

Oh, how sweet it is to be A. Big Shot Attorney. He walks down the hall and shouts in his paralegal's general direction: "I want that latest production organized and indexed by 5:00 today." That's great. However, it would be physically impossible for one person to read and analyze the 30,000-page document dump that A. Big Shot Attorney is referencing. Lawyers need to understand that tasks do not get finished as quickly as they can spout them out, but they don't care. Paralegals are not secret wizards or genies who can make wishes happen upon command. The lawyers are completely oblivious of the ripple effects of what they do to their paralegals. For instance, picture a lawyer reviewing exhibits for trial. Every single time they change something about an exhibit, the paralegal must update every attorney's trial notebook, the master copies traveling to court, the original exhibit that will be tendered to the court, the firm's electronic database of exhibits, and then notify the tech team of the change so they do not put the old exhibit up on the screen in front of a jury. To move one piece of paper takes the lawyer probably a fraction of a second, but it probably means a twenty-minute task for the paralegal, and quite possibly even longer.

The lawyer sits back in his office and says: "Send a records request out for BLANK." Again, giving assignments takes literally a few seconds. The paralegal has to verify the facility's contact information and format a request. Yes, the firm has model language and a template to use, but the paralegal still has to read it every time and make sure it makes sense for the current objective. It takes time to save a copy of the final executed request to the file, and to update the records tracking spreadsheet so there is a reminder to make sure a timely response is received. It is a simple task, but it is not a mindless task. After it is complete, it takes a few minutes to get transitioned into another task.

Once, I even got called into work on a Sunday by a notorious jackass. I had just started working for a new firm and I thought the guy's reputation had to have been exaggerated for story-telling purposes. I was wrong. You know what the guy wanted me to do? Go get his lunch! He did not want me to do any paralegal work whatsoever. He just needed his sandwich (no tomatoes, for God's sakes, do not ever EVER get the tomatoes if you value your life and the lives of your children), cookie, and a Coke. Besides chewing copious amounts of tobacco, his next favorite activity was to yell for me over the entire office (especially in front of his clients) to go and fetch him things. "MINION! GET IN HERE!"

I WANT IT Syndrome can also refer to the need to propound impossible questions to the paralegal. My favorite type of question is asking me to testify to the scope of someone else's knowledge. For instance, after I have responded to a normal question, perhaps regarding some documents we produced in response to a Request for Production of Documents, the attorney might ask me something along the lines of: "Well, does ___ know about this report?"

I cannot possibly know the scope of someone else's knowledge, and no one else can either. This question drives me crazy because it is so stupid and ridiculous. I usually just responded with: "I cannot say with any accuracy what ___ knows." It is the same thing when they ask me what other people have done. The proper response is: "Maybe you should ask ___ what he did."

EXHIBIT 24

NO MONEY FOR FILE CLERKS OR BONUSES. BUT PLENTY OF MONEY FOR CLOWNS.

On xxxx, Other Minion Paralegal wrote to A. Big Shot Attorney:

I haven't had much time to search for a file clerk. I've contacted a staffing agency and they can get us a file clerk for $15/hour, we typically pay $10/hr. The file clerk works 20 hrs/wk so it would be an additional $100/wk in expense. Can we go this route? The filing is really getting backed up at this point and we need someone in here quickly who knows what they are doing.

From: A. Big Shot Attorney
To: Other Minion Paralegal
Subject: File Clerk

No, we need to fill that position as we have in the past. We don't have unlimited funds to continue to increase expenses. Take the time to get someone hired. There are three great places to find someone.

This email came right before the firm spent hundreds of dollars on a surprise clown for A. Big Shot Attorney's birthday, and failed to pay staff bonuses. Morale pretty much went straight down the toilet after that incident. The below email explains why it is so important that we have a good file clerk:

From: Other Minion Paralegal
To: All Minions
Subject: Filing

All, I cannot stress enough to everyone how important the filing is to this firm. Documents just HAVE TO BE put in the proper file. I cannot go to court and have A. big Shot Attorney turn around and ask me for a document and I go right to where it should be and it not be there. This CANNOT happen to anyone in this firm. Please take your filing seriously and pay attention when doing it.

The two oldest files we have are SEVEN and NINE years old. YEARS and YEARS of filing with YEARS and YEARS of numerous hands on it. Everyone MUST follow the same procedures and PAY ATTENTION when it comes to filing. We ALL MUST be consistent and diligent with the filing.

There are many things we can't control when it comes to our cases and trial, but the filing certainly can be controlled.

None of us should ever have to sit in a courtroom with everyone waiting on a document that can't be found because it is misfiled.

EXHIBIT 25

YOU HAVEN'T SACRIFICED ENOUGH

From: Minion Paralegal
To: Boyfriend
Subject: Life on Friday

Not feeling good at all. Can't breathe, sore throat, etc. Made it home from work and been relaxing for a good two hours. Total survival mode at work. Sad today because not being heard there. It does not matter what I do, they do not want to listen to anything I have to say. My job is to fetch, not to think and convey those thoughts. To be seen, but not heard, like all good servants and children.

Thinking today of our deceased client on my way in to work, and how it turns out that I lived about .04 miles from him some years ago. My apartment was just around the corner. My grocery store was his grocery store. There was a cafe I used to eat at all the time in that shopping center. If I would get out of paralegal classes early, I would go in there and treat myself. I had a dedicated server, it seemed. I can't remember his name now, but he was always there and we got to be on good terms. So good in fact, that I knew he was in a drug rehab for using heroin. One night in the rain, they were closing up, and I saw him begin to walk in the parking lot - not towards any car. I yelled out to him, and he told me he just lived across the street so I drove him. All the way to the back of the complex (where I later found out the drug rehab apartments were), and I remember thinking how crazy it was back there - people milling all around, etc. Just a really crazy vibe. And I don't know it for certain, and I can't prove it, but I feel that my server was our client's roommate. Even if he wasn't, he certainly would have known who our client was.

Memories. Five years ago. Things will come back to you sometimes and slam you right up against the wall. And I wonder - how close did I get to him? Did I stand by him in the store? Did I pass him on the road? Did I deliver his roommate home one night in the rain? I don't know. It is a weird feeling. My connection to the dead man. There are no coincidences. Unless there are.

It is a story and piece of my history that has nothing to do with a lawsuit, and so when I tried to tell the team about it, as I was walking out the door this afternoon, I got shut down. And the story was delivered not even half told, as they killed my spirit in the quiet little way that they do on most days. Not by yelling at me, or abusing me. But by pretending I don't exist. By refusing to hear me. "Silly, Minion. She thinks she has something to say to us." And so time passes on. And I waste away another day. Quietly, and all to myself.

And here is what I said to them after I'd finally had enough of the insanity:

From: Minion Paralegal
To: Big Shot Attorneys
Subject: Resignation Letter

Thank you for letting me be of service to you and your clients over the years. However, I am no longer suited to be a full-time salaried employee and here are a few reasons why I know this:

Why I am a Bad Employee

- You mentioned there may be some problems with me being a threat or being received by some of my so-called peers in the office. I just don't care if someone is threatened by my high performance, or is not ready to receive me. That smacks of what my father would just call a sorry person. I personally desire to be around people who are smarter than I am and who have something to teach me. I am not interested in being around people who want to drag me down or impede my progress. I need to be around people who want to rise to my level, or who are better than me and want to help me rise to theirs. I am not interested in having to engage in weird psychological warfare with co-workers who always seem to have something crazy going on that interferes with their job. I just don't care. This makes me a bad employee.

- I want to engage in activities one time, and get them right whenever possible. I want to act with purpose, efficiently, and accurately. I get extremely frustrated when I am faced with a loss of time situation. My thinking is that I don't want to waste my time anymore; it depresses me and hurts my spirit. Some of my co-workers may think: "Whatever. We're getting paid to be here." I still think: "If you didn't want to file this motion, why did you have me spend six hours marking exhibits, copying exhibits, and scanning them?" This is not just emotionally and psychologically draining, but this is taking time away from other clients that need real work done on their cases, meanwhile wasting tangible resources such as copy toner, exhibit stickers, and paper. These resources are fairly expensive just to waste. This makes me a bad employee, and I need to get out before I lose the fight and turn into a mindless zombie who only cares about getting a paycheck for moving paper from one side of the office to another.

- The thought of preparing for another trial on a case I didn't have from the beginning makes me want to drive my car into oncoming traffic. It is just way too hard on me and emotionally taxing and stressful. Further, I do not personally find it motivating anymore to make personal sacrifices without any additional tangible benefit other than getting to keep my job. That isn't a reward anymore. It is a prison.

And I walked away, battered and beaten, humiliated and exhausted. With an unfettered belief that I would live happily ever after. I finally knew who I was and there was no one on this earth who could steal that sense of self from me. I was a warrior.

FIVE

SURVIVAL TIPS

If for some reason you find yourself stuck in a law firm and can't get out, I offer my best coping mechanisms and advice from the trenches to you as follows:

1. Do not get too friendly with your co-workers. You want to be helpful, trusted, and respected. You get that by going about your business quietly, and volunteering a little bit to take over things. You do not get respected by allowing people to take advantage of you. It is to your advantage to be a little bit scary to your co-workers. This means they will leave you the hell alone for the most part.

2. Keep your mouth shut. You don't talk in the elevator about anything other than the weather or what movie you last saw. Same goes for the kitchen and the bathrooms. You don't tell what you know. Stay quiet and everyone else will tell you things about everyone else. Knowledge is power. Especially when it comes to making sure you swing those vacation days with the Administrator!

3. Always eat breakfast and keep healthy snacks in your bag or stashed in your desk.

4. Take your full lunch break every damn day unless you are paid to work through it.

5. Set your boundaries in the beginning for control of your own life. If you are signed up to take a class twice a week at 6:00 p.m., you have to leave at 5:00 to make your class. You do not have to tell them why you cannot stay late. All they need to know is that you can't do it.

6. However bad it seems, it is just a job. This will not be the only job you are ever offered in your entire life. Also, it is okay to quit if you are miserable. Your suffering is not going to equal a big prize at the end.

7. Sometimes, you have to let the associates fail on their own without intervening to save them. This is the only way they will come to respect you.

8. Do not sacrifice your relationships or your health for a paycheck. One day when you realize that no one even knows who you are anymore (yourself, chief among these people) you will understand this.

9. Do not expect anything from anyone. This only leads to a sense of entitlement and that is not going to be pretty. You signed up for a paycheck. You are staff, you don't get part of the take.

10. If you are a real square, call out sick every now and then and give yourself a "me" day. Trust me on this one.

CLOSING REMARKS

Can you check your ego and personal pride and handle working with attorneys? It is exhausting work, certainly. No matter who you work for, you must always keep the attorney's delicate ego in mind. He will believe that he is the smartest, most capable lawyer that ever walked the planet. You will be expected to act as if this were so. Can you do that?

If you are terribly unlucky, like I was at the very last law firm I ever worked for, you might get stuck with a bad apple. Not only did I have a Dirty Old Man showing me his "I Love My Penis!" cream, I also had a horrible male boss who yelled at me in front of co-workers and even clients to "Get in here!" After I read Bob Sutton's The *No Asshole Rule*, I was determined to leave that job as soon as possible. This guy was a barking dog and I frequently had to bite my tongue and sit on my hands to keep from throwing things at his tobacco-chewing face. It was time to refuse to be a human punching bag, and hopefully to make a statement to the firm and my other female co-workers that this behavior is not acceptable.

In the end, you may be lucky enough to work with a group of people who aren't rude or mean to your face. However, they will still view you as beneath them. They will leave for lunch and never include you, they will write emails to each other referring to you as "staff" instead of by your name, and they will say things to their peers such as "I'll have my paralegal jump and do ___." If you can swallow that, my hat is off to you. I wanted more for myself than to be called "staff." I wanted to spend my days doing good work and lining my own pockets from the fruits of my labor. I was not prepared to make unlimited sacrifices without any additional personal gain to contributing to someone else's company. When you work for someone else, ultimately you are always expendable. It does not matter how good you are. Someone else will always be along to replace you, and probably at a cheaper rate, at that. When you leave, you pack up your little photographs and it will be as though you were never even there at all.

Perhaps that is the best thing to believe – that you were never really there at all.

www.ingramcontent.com/pod-product-compliance
Lightning Source LLC
Chambersburg PA
CBHW081008170526
45158CB00010B/2956